Online Afterlives

Online Afterlives

Immortality, Memory, and Grief in Digital Culture

Davide Sisto

Translated by Bonnie McClellan-Broussard

The MIT Press

Cambridge, Massachusetts | London, England

This book was set in Stone Serif and Stone Sans by Westchester Publishing Services. Printed and bound in the United States of America.

Library of Congress Cataloging-in-Publication Data

Names: Sisto, Davide, 1978- author. | McClellan-Broussard, Bonnie, translator.
Title: Online afterlives : immortality, memory, and grief in digital culture / Davide Sisto ; translated by Bonnie McClellan-Broussard.
Other titles: Morte si fa social. English
Description: Cambridge, Massachusetts : The MIT Press, [2020] | "Original Italian edition: ©2018 Bollati Boringhiere editore, Torino"--Title page verso. | Includes bibliographical references and index.
Identifiers: LCCN 2019058436 | ISBN 9780262539395 (paperback)
Subjects: LCSH: Death--Social aspects. | Online social networks--Social aspects. | Internet--Social aspects.
Classification: LCC HQ1073 .S5413 2020 | DDC 306.9--dc23
LC record available at https://lccn.loc.gov/2019058436

10 9 8 7 6 5 4 3 2 1

Contents

Introduction

Death Returns to the Web

When I turned on my smartphone on the morning of November 14, 2014, I got a notification from Facebook. It was reminding me to send a birthday message to my friend Alessandro. *Contribuisci a rendere unica la sua giornata* (Help to make his day special) appeared beside his profile picture. All of this was unremarkable, except for the fact that Alessandro was dead. He had died the previous summer. For a few seconds I was bewildered, unable to fully comprehend the disconnect. My first instinct was to go to his Facebook profile page. I started looking through his daily posts, reading some of his past status updates, looking at the photographs he had posted. Then I went straight to our private conversations on Facebook Messenger and WhatsApp. Alessandro was an emerging film director who had enjoyed some international success with a documentary about the experiences of albinos in Tanzania. His lively Facebook page bore witness to the many trips he'd made to different places around the world over the years. And then, suddenly, *silence*. A void that brought together Alessandro's last "living" update with the first posthumous memorial post written by a grieving friend.

All of this was both disconcerting and emotionally powerful for me. It forced me to reflect on how death, so often kept at arm's length from our everyday lives, is foisted peremptorily upon us on social networks, chat threads, and the internet in general.

The presence of a deceased person's Facebook profile in the midst of the profiles of the living is a phenomenon that can in no way be compared to, for example, a visit to a grave (or other such memorial place). Nor is it comparable to pulling out a photograph that you've kept in an album tucked away on a shelf. We have come to expect the traces of a dead person's life to settle into fixed spaces and objects, or memories of their family members and friends. And we assume their legacy—for example, the lessons they passed on or the example they set as parents—will, one way or the other, come to shape the lives of those they were close to. So consider now how a person's digital "footprint" is fated to wander aimlessly, perhaps eternally, indiscriminately confronting anyone with whom they may have had even the briefest interaction or slightest acquaintance. These days, we can encounter traces of the dead when we type their names into a search engine or, as in my case, when we receive a notification about a friend's birthday. In computing terms, every "random spider" or web crawler that systematically browses the web, in order to create an index, sucks up this "dead data," locking it away in a kind of digital mausoleum that is always accessible to living users.[1]

The South Korean philosopher Byung-Chul Han, one of the foremost critics of digital culture, argues that while the internet resembles Jeremy Bentham's panopticon in many ways, *unlike* Bentham's panopticon—which was devoid of an effective registration system—the internet makes it possible to systematically record our entire lives and make them accessible through its multiform digital networks.[2] In other words, we are all fated to become *digital ghosts*, trapped in posterity, without our consent, forever digitally undead. These enduring online records are paradoxically a reminder of both the inevitability of death and the impossibility of the traces of our lives ever being truly erased.

One of the purposes of death studies is to help people accept death as an integral part of life and provide support to those who need to find a way to mourn. I wonder then if digital culture doesn't unintentionally offer an opportunity to those of us who, over the last few decades, have been trying to offset the sociocultural denial of death in the West?[3] In the West, we continue to resist the reality of mortality and we keep the dead, literally and figuratively, at a distance. After all, to talk about death, let's say during a lunch with friends or on a TV chat show, is often still considered taboo, macabre, or in bad taste.

We struggle even in our attempts to discuss death purely in terms of it being a biomedical phenomenon, as the American surgeon Atul Gawande makes clear in his bestseller *Being Mortal: Medicine and What Matters in the End*.[4] We need only consider the results of a recent piece of scientific research carried out in Australia on a sample of more than three thousand people from thirty-nine different countries that analyzed the linguistic expressions commonly used to describe a person's death. They clearly show how deeply rooted is the tendency to name anything but *death itself*. In addition to the idiomatic and ubiquitous "passed away," "passed on," and "departed," an impressive variety of euphemisms, metaphors, and paraphrases exists to allow us to avoid uttering the word "dead" in the process of relaying the news of the death of a loved one.

Several English-language idioms stand out for their black humor: *wrong side of the grass* and *taking a dirt nap* are just two examples. Many paraphrases have specific cultural and historical origins: for example, *shuffled off this mortal coil* is a well-known quote taken from Shakespeare's *Hamlet*. *Six feet under* is a phrase that dates back to 1665 and indicates the need to bury plague victims as deeply as possible. Recently, this phrase has been used as both the name of a death metal band and the title of a very successful American TV series about, unsurprisingly, thanatological topics. *Promoted to glory* is a metaphor used by the Salvation Army when referring to victims of a war. There's also no shortage of references in local slang, like *carked it*: in Australia "cark" is the call of the crow, an animal whose association with death and cemeteries hardly needs to be pointed out. Then there's *brown bread*, used in Cockney rhyming slang, the patois of the Greater London area, simply because it rhymes with *dead*.

Linguistic formulas also clearly evoke the illusion of a life without death. One commonly heard in Italy is *stroncato da un male incurabile* (literally, "struck down by an incurable disease"), used to indicate a death due to a malign tumor, such as cancer, without having to refer explicitly to "cancer" or "death." The Italian verb *stroncare*—"to cut off" or "to strike down"—immediately brings to mind a violent action that, without prior warning, interrupts the ordinary course of life. What is actually *striking down* the life could be a tumor, an "incurable disease," which evokes the idea of a defeat following a desperate battle against an enemy invading from the outside. The surgeon Alberta Ferrari, after hearing this phrase used for the umpteenth time to refer to the death of the Italian actress Virna Lisi, launched an appeal on the pages of the popular weekly *L'Espresso* to completely eliminate it as a phrase because it's both antiquated and, above all, inadequate for an authentic and nuanced understanding of death's role in our lives.[5]

> It's a "Mr. Death" or something. He's come about *the reaping*? I don't think we need any at the moment!

This absurd one-liner uttered by one of the characters in the Monty Python film *The Meaning of Life* (1983) in response to the Grim Reaper when it comes knocking at their door—a visit prompted by the effects of a salmon mousse that has gone bad—quite accurately describes our troubled relationship with death.

Yet these strategies we adopt in our day-to-day language to avoid thoughts of mortality are frustrated by communication technologies such as wireless, the cloud, and broadband, which make the online world profoundly pervasive. And death is everywhere in the digital environment. It's in our social networks, embedded in our selfies on Instagram, popular hashtags, live-streamed amateur videos, not to mention on news sites, blogs, and a multiplicity of other websites. When we consider the ubiquity of death online in comparison with the way in which it's erased and ignored off-line, we bear witness to a chaotic fluctuation between a healthy rediscovery of the role that death plays in our lives and a media-driven sensationalism, which ultimately serves only to scavenge off of and trivialize death.

Eran Alfonta, CEO of the Israel-based startup company Willook, is the inventor of If I Die (http://ifidie.net/), an app that offers the possibility of preparing farewell video messages and written texts to be published on Facebook after one's death. He argues that these days we are on Facebook all our lives—and even before we are born, in the images of prenatal sonograms shared by our parents. We are born on Facebook, we grow up on Facebook, and we get married and divorced on Facebook. This is all documented every day with messages, photographs, and videos. So then why should there be anything strange about dying on Facebook? Indeed, it's surprising that social network operators, at least so far, have underestimated the opportunities provided by this unavoidable aspect of our existence. Whether they like to think about it or not, their users, in addition to flirting, arguing, and sharing fake news, will, inevitably, get sick and die.

"Death is a part of life and life has become digital." This is how Stacey Pitsillides, an English design researcher, introduces Digital Death (http://digitaldeath) on her website, where she gathers articles, statistics, interviews, and videos focusing on the link between digital culture and death—with specific attention given to the changes images have undergone in the transition from analog to digital.[6] If death is a part of life and life has become digital, it is inevitable that death has also become digital, combining the private with the public, the individual with the collective, and the real with the virtual. We are now experiencing a rediscovery of its *communal* dimension. This aspect was lost in the twentieth century with the increasing isolation of the terminally ill in hospitals, the dead in cemeteries—so often situated in a secluded corner of the city—and the mourners confined to their homes, the only place where they are allowed to express openly their grief and suffering—and that only temporarily.

Alfonta and Pitsillides highlight a peculiar characteristic of today's society: with the popularization of the internet and the subsequent development of social networks, we are learning to live in two "homes" simultaneously. The *traditional* home, to which we return physically every day, leaving our workday stress behind; and the *virtual* home, which collects and distributes our data and our digital objects—a home that we often only truly leave when we're asleep (and not necessarily even then!) This second home, hybrid and unearthly, hyper-present and eternal, archives the continually expanding digital lives of every internet user and records a significant portion of an individual's existence. With just a simple mobile device, everyone can present themselves to the public on a daily basis. On websites, blogs, chats, forums, and social networks, there is a ceaseless stream of tastes, passions, prejudices, beliefs, decisions, boasts, and experiences.

Yet this ephemera, seemingly lost in the continuous flow of information, does leave an indelible trace. Just think about Pinterest, one of the largest image archives on the internet. It registers onto its server every single image published on its users' "mood boards," which are then linked back to the images' original sources, be they stock library images or private family photos. It indirectly functions like a library of preexisting images.

As Luciano Floridi argues, it is a mistake to believe that the virtual home leads to unqualified advantages for the traditional home. It is not simply a cross between "an adaptation of human agents to digital environments" and "a form of postmodern neo-colonization of digital environments by human agents." The two homes, online and off-line, are not superimposed. With the unceasing evolution of the web, their boundaries are increasingly blurred. "The digital-online world is spilling over into the analogue-offline world and merging with it" which, Floridi argues, gives us all an "*onlife experience*." It makes no sense to consider these as two separate, parallel worlds.[7]

The awareness of being *onlife*, which is to say to be living in these two homes concurrently—the first predominantly private, the second interactive and intersubjective, both of which mingle with each other and are interdependent to such a degree that they are barely distinguishable—involves a radical rethinking of our public and private ties with death and mourning, with memory and oblivion, with funeral rites and grief, and with our own vision of *the corpse*. Every day we contribute more to the building of a complex digital panorama that comprises our personality traits and socio-cultural relations—and we share it in a public arena. Can we really be surprised at the suggestion of our own online immortality? In just a few years, Generation X—those people born between 1965 and 1980—will be the last generation to have lived in an era without computers, mobile devices and, most importantly, without an internet connection. The near future will be populated exclusively by digital natives; those who have become used to managing, from the very first years of their lives, these two increasingly integrated home environments.

This means—for Floridi—that we will become, if we haven't already, *inforgs*, "informational organisms, mutually connected and embedded in an informational environment (the infosphere), which we share with other informational agents, both natural and artificial, that also process information logically and autonomously."[8] Living as informational organisms, within an infosphere in which natural beings and artificial agents share each other's spaces and form inter-connected identities, as individual fragments of a participatory All-One, means facing unprecedented circumstances relative to the consciousness of mortality, management of an individual's belongings, and the desire to be remembered. But also, as we shall see, in relation to a concrete hope of immortality.

The "fourth revolution," which foresees the continual delegation of our memories and recollections to artificial agents, while far from opening up posthuman scenarios of biotechnological transformation of the corporeality (the famous *Homo cyborg*), does offer new solutions to and opportunities for our complicated relationship with the end of life and the passage of time. If we don't wish to be unprepared for the return of death—often as sudden as it is unforeseen—in the public space, the time has come to become aware of these opportunities and to address them with full knowledge of the facts.

Digital Death Manager: A Twenty-First-Century Profession

In 2018 *Time* magazine recognized *Döstädning* as a trending profession and predicted that it would continue to grow for years to come. *Döstädning* is a Swedish term that can be translated into English as *death cleaning*. In practice, this is the organization and putting into order of one's own physical home in view of one's death.[9] When someone dies, there is the risk that their most precious objects will die with them; the very objects that are an extension of an individual's own unique personality. The uniqueness of any given physical object—existing in one place and time, with its own fragility, subjected to the wear and tear of time—makes the bond established with its owner irreproducible and singular; therefore, the integral aspect of the object is its story rather than its object-ness. In their own way, those personal objects that do remain after an individual's death cannot help but preserve the memory of the deceased.[10]

For these reasons, *death cleaning* reaffirms our understanding of the relationships that link life with death, because it presents us with the reality of what is left behind after we are gone. All of our letters, photographs, clothing, jewelry, etc. will continue to exist after we die. Putting everything in order in advance, eliminating what is unnecessary (unwanted gifts, clothes we've never worn, things we've never used) and organizing that which we want to keep on living in the hands of those we love, means attentively considering the sense of our own passage through the world, dealing with our fear of death, and thinking rationally about what of ourselves we want to leave for posterity. It puts us face to face with the uselessness of keeping too many things, more often than not superfluous, and the need to avoid forcing our relatives to make emotionally difficult decisions about what to keep and what to throw away.

In some cases, the rarity of an object, and its deep connection to a loved one, puts friends and relatives in an uncomfortable position because they believe that using that object would indicate a lack of respect, or even a betrayal of the history embedded within it. Throwing it away doesn't resolve the issue. It is the unique and deep connection with our loved ones that makes the inheritance of an object a token of the spiritual survival of a finite life. As Novalis said in the Romantic era, "We seek the absolute everywhere and only ever find things."[11]

The same rationale also needs to be applied to the virtual home with its *digital objects*, the quantities of which are incomparably higher than those of physical objects. Passwords and information related to the dozens or even hundreds of accounts a person owns (and sometimes forgets about), assorted photographs, videos, letters, and narratives that, being part of a personal digital memory, differ from physical objects only in the way they are created, kept, shared, and transmitted. Because they may exist in an offline computer, within the context of social networks, associated with an email address or in a cloud storage service (Dropbox, iCloud Drive, Google Drive, etc.) and almost never printed, digital objects are never irreproducible. In fact, there may be multiple copies stored for an unlimited time, as well as saved simultaneously in several virtual locations by an incalculable number of people who, in turn, can reproduce them infinitely. So theoretically, they can last indefinitely, be available on multiple online platforms, and spread virally. And yet they are also at risk of being forever inaccessible if they are protected by passwords that nobody knows, except the late owner.

Indeed, a few months ago, when I was on the train from Turin to Milan, a man sitting near me noticed that the bag containing his laptop had been stolen. "I've lost my whole life!" He hadn't had the foresight to save the documents that were on his PC to a backup storage device or to a cloud storage service and, consequently, a great deal of his private and business life had evaporated in a single instant. In a certain sense, in the course of a few brief minutes, he found himself "evicted" from his virtual home.

In their book, *Your Digital Afterlife: When Facebook, Flickr and Twitter Are Your Estate, What's Your Legacy?*, Evan Carroll and John Romano highlight the changes that have occurred in the transition between digital and physical objects through a comparison between the letters sent to the family of an American soldier in the Vietnam War in 1968 and the emails sent to the family of another American solider during the Iraq War in 2004. The first letters were subject to lengthy delays and the incumbent risks of physical mail (letters getting damaged or lost); and the second letters were subject to the terms of service applicable to that specific email client.[12] In light of such changes, the New York think tank sparks & honey, an agency that focuses on monitoring new trends in technology, posits that one of the eight new future jobs that will be established by 2025 will be that of digital death manager. These experts on the interaction between digital culture and the end of life who, by virtue of their knowledge and aptitude as "virtual undertakers," will help the inhabitants of the infosphere

- be aware of what could happen to data and to digital information and objects after an individual's death, in order to take appropriate decisions beforehand;
- understand the effects that such data, information, and objects will have on them later and on the memories that the individual who has died will leave as an inheritance;

- think about the transformations undergone by the *memento mori* at both the individual and the social level;
- imagine new and hypothetical scenarios of immortality;
- avoid neglecting, over the course of their lives, the effects caused by the loss of personal data, digital objects, and information (for example, when a computer breaks or is stolen and the owner hasn't taken the precaution of backing up on alternate storage media or using a cloud storage service).

Ultimately, the first task of digital death managers will be to provide support in organizing the material that has been shared online, in order to arrive at a clear awareness of what will happen to our digital lives once we are no longer able to manage this material ourselves. Second, these people will deal with the consequences of an individual's digital survival after death. Last, they will plan and manage the mourning, weighing the opportunities and problems that result from the daily use of the web. Is this not precisely what the Swedish death cleaners do?

Digital death managers, using the opportunities provided by digital technology, and combining practical archival know-how with theoretical literacy, are therefore professional *thanatologists*.

Indeed, the demand for practical thanatology is already quite evident today. There is the iPhone app WeCroak, for instance, invented by two thirtysomething freelancers, Ian Thomas and Hansa Bergwall, which—playfully—warns us five times a day not to forget that we're going to die. The app, inspired by a Bhutanese song about the inevitability of death, while reminding us that our lives could end at any moment, perhaps also provides us with the opportunity to reevaluate the choices we make in our daily lives. In this way we might learn to be like Charles Bukowski, who kept "death" in his left pocket, always ready to take it out at any time and talk to it: "Hello baby, how you doing? When you coming for me? I'll be ready."[13] Or we might avoid the craven behavior of Victor who, in Javier Marías's novel *Tomorrow in the Battle Think on Me*, is so overwhelmed when his married lover Marta suddenly dies in his arms that he runs away in a panic without notifying anyone—even leaving her young son asleep in the apartment with his mother's corpse.

In this book I will describe those special characteristics that tie digital culture to death and analyze the unprecedented social, cultural, and philosophical scenarios that spring up online, reintroducing death as a topic for public discourse. If the innovations introduced by digital culture offset and reflect our off-line behaviors, I hope to show how a society that is willing to engage with death and mortality is a more balanced and mature one, better equipped to face the challenges of everyday life.

Chi muore si rivede (Those who die are seen again)

In 1985, Vilém Flusser argued that "the real intention of telematics is to become immortal."[14] He was predicting our ability to store our information and memories on intangible media—such as electromagnetic fields—and the radical reduction in our use of, and interest in, physical media. Flusser gives the example of the cyclical life of a leather shoe: an everyday object that originates in, and, ultimately, returns to, the natural world once it is worn out and discarded by its owner. Circumventing the cyclical path of the shoe, electronic images in the telematic age are instead "reservoirs of information, that serve our immortality."[15]

Twelve years later, in 1997, in an article published in the scientific journal *Death Studies*, Carla Sofka coined the term *thanatechnology* to describe technological mechanisms with which to access information concerning a deceased person, both for the clinical practice of, and for activities broadly related to, death studies and thanatological research.[16] These mechanisms allow new possibilities for multimedia narratives and funereal commemorations. Even in the late 1990s—a time when the internet was mainly a place for research and a means of archiving, used primarily for consulting information rather than interactive participation—digital environments dedicated to mourning and to commemorating the dead were present in embryonic form: virtual cemeteries, funeral rituals, and cybernetic obituaries. The first virtual cemetery, the World Wide Cemetery (https://cemetery.org/) was created on April 28, 1995, by Canadian Mike Kibbee, soon after he discovered that he was ill with cancer, with the goal of creating an online platform for memorializing the dead.

Now, more than twenty years after Sofka's intuition— and with the popular spread of web 2.0 and (almost) 3.0, as a place for exchange, sharing, and interaction—the frequency with which we refer to concepts such as "digital patrimony," "digital heritage" and "digital immortality" is increasing. If you search for terms like "social media and death" or simply "digital death," you'll find many articles and multidisciplinary studies. For several years, the International Death Online Research Symposium has been held in different locations and involved dozens of scholars from all over the world, all engaged in researching the relationship between digital culture and the end of life. One such example is Death Goes Digital (http://www.deathgoesdigital .com/), whose manager, Peter Billingham, presents himself as a digital death advisor, helping funerary industry practitioners deal with the problems inherent in dying in today's digital society, especially with reference to contemporary funeral rites.

In trying to understand thanatechnology, it's tempting to include any attempt to try to make sense of loss and mourning through online engagement. Add to that the fact that the immense amount of material produced online means that it's difficult to achieve a productive balance between legal considerations and what needs to be preserved.

The concept of thanatechnology is primarily linked to two specific characteristics of digital culture, brought clearly into focus by John Durham Peters in his book *Speaking into the Air: A History of the Idea of Communication*: the *ease* with which the living can mingle with communicable traces of the dead; and the *difficulty* of distinguishing communication at a distance (like chats, messaging, and emails) from communication with the dead.[17] In order to understand these two characteristics, it will be necessary to take a step back to consider the specific conditions that are part of the experience of images of death.

Present in Absence: Photography and Death

If an irrevocable absence—a presence that vanishes forever—are the first consequences of a person's death, the status of the dead is nevertheless defined by a particular paradox: once the funeral rites are observed, the dead become the "incarnation of an absent presence." They are absent but present, or rather are *present in the absence*. They depart yet, at the same time, remain as a permanent remnant. In other words, they become a double that "differs from its living twin without becoming someone else."[18]

The paradox between the presence and absence of the dead is the direct result of, on the one hand, awareness of the hopelessly empty place that is left by that person in the public sphere, which any relative or friend would want at all costs to fill, and on the other, the inability of the living to personally know death themselves. From the perspective of the living, death can only ever be a reminder of itself: or in other words, a representation or *image* of its ontological reality. Indeed, *image* is deeply connected with death; created to extend the living memory of the dead and alleviate the suffering linked to grief. The true meaning of the image is provided by what, having become absent, can *only* remain present in terms of representation. Just think about the relationship between the corpse and a person's physical body: the corpse fully coincides with the person but, at the same time, it is nothing more than a residual image that reminds us of their physical being—an inert representation, because there is no longer any life in it. However, this coincidence between death and image also implies their innate separateness. For the well-being of the living and for a successful completion of mourning, the image must be separated from the corpse.

"The work of mourning," writes the French philosopher Régis Debray, "involves going through the process of constructing an image of the other that works to liberate (us and them)....Like a baby recognizing its own limbs in a mirror for the first time, we (the living) counter death and decomposition by using the image to recompose (the body)....It (the image) comes to us from beyond the tomb and we use it to ensure that our ancestor remains there, passive and fixed; trapped in a stable object, so that his wandering soul cannot return to harass us. We cannot rid ourselves of his double without materializing it."[19]

The separation of the corpse from its image, through which we counter its decomposition with a recomposition, establishes the substantial difference between the dead and the not-dead. The image is made separate from the deceased as a new personification, which varies according to the culture to which they belonged, and the dead are then born into their new posthumous lives. In this way the gruesome vision of purification is avoided and, along with it, the confusion between the pure and impure once the body of the beloved, devoid of life, gradually begins to decay.

As thanatologist Tony Walter argues, digital communication technology has not profoundly redefined the nature and extent of the social presence of the dead. The images of the dead have been present among the living throughout history, in books and legends, in oracles and myths, within our dreams and various funeral rites, through historic monuments, sculptures, masks, and painted portraits. And especially in statues.

"Where do statues come to us from?" asks Michel Serres. "They come back. Gods, heroes or men, great or false, resurrect as ghosts. Phantoms that rise from second funerals, at the end of all rotting. Pure remains of their liquefied flesh. Statues come to us from that first gruesome technique, exercised on that first object, a universal practice, characteristic of every culture, from which the origin of every technology emerges in the human race."[20]

Almost every technology available to humans throughout history has been used to ensure the presence of the dead in society and, at the same time, to prevent the return of their restless, possibly dangerous, spirits to the world of the living. However, current information technology, with its constant innovations, has the benefit of offering more options for this kind of social presence; new kinds of social links and symbolic rituals. Most importantly, the more specialized and complex this information becomes, the lower the risk that the afterlives of the dead—especially as time passes and their friends and relatives die also—will fall into eternal oblivion.

Although this might not always be the case, as we will analyze shortly.

In the last few centuries, the dissociation of the image
from the dead is realized most starkly in the custom of plac-
ing photographs of the deceased on headstones above their
graves. This ritual has a dual function: it symbolically provides the deceased with an "immortal body," which will
preserve and represent them indefinitely, and it helps those
who are grieving forget about the gradual decomposition
that the corpse is undergoing inside the grave. Photography, in this case, performs the role of appropriating the—
now lost—existence of the deceased, by combining the need
for the body to be transformed into a fixed image and the
need for that image to be made incarnate.[21] Photography,
in this instance, allows us to lie to ourselves; a symbolic
embalming process that keeps the biological effects of death
at a distance while maintaining a presence of those who
have become absent. The full convergence of the *I*—brittle
and changeable—and the *image*—heavy and static—seems
momentarily possible.

The dead as the presence of an absence made incarnate
begins to become clear. And photographs, as the culmination of our centuries-old representational and pictorial tradition, have really performed—especially during the twentieth
century—as Susan Sontag writes, the task of creating "the
inventory of mortality." Rather than the hand that cuts out
a paper *silhouette* of the deceased with a simple movement
of the fingers, the camera *immortalizes* on film the people
and things that, with their shadows, are irrefutably there in

that given instant, at a specific age in their lives and often placed together by chance. In the next instant, they disperse and never again come together or return to the same place. They die in the moment in which they are photographed. The instant immortalized contains within it the absences of before and after, the void that passing time places between the presence and the absence of someone who is no longer there, the randomness of the specific situation, the nostalgia tied to the weight of the past. "Photographs," concludes Sontag, "state the innocence, the vulnerability of lives heading toward their own destruction, and this link between photography and death haunts all photographs of people."[22] With photography, it is no longer possible to abandon one's own image, which appropriates the life it has recorded of the body portrayed, keeping every movement and every characteristic of it as a memory.

For this reason, Roland Barthes sees photographers as "agents of death": removed from the public space in which we live, death survives in the image that, reproduced, wants to preserve life. Living images of a dead thing: the stillness of photography takes advantage of the confusion between the concepts of real and alive. While attesting that the object has been real, at the same time the photograph "surreptitiously induces belief that it is alive, because of that delusion which makes us attribute to Reality an absolutely superior, somehow eternal value; but by shifting this reality to the past ("this-has-been"), the photograph suggests that it is already dead."[23] In the three practices, which are the objective of photography—to do, to undergo, to look—are the central point of the dialectic between real and living: in the encounter between the one who "does" (the photographer or *operator*), the one who "looks" (the *spectator*), and the one who "undergoes" (the photographed or *spectrum*), the symbiosis between simulacrum and the *spectrum* is realized, given that—within the image that immortalizes it—there is the posthumous life of the deceased, his re-composition. This is why, according to Barthes, a relationship between photography and theater can be established in relation to death: if in a theatrical production the actors play the dead, for which they put on the makeup and costumes of a body that is dead and alive at the same time, "however 'lifelike' we strive to make it ... Photography is a kind of primitive theatre, a kind of *Tableau Vivant*, a figuration of the motionless and made-up face beneath which we see the dead."[24]

The photographic image is, as Jacques Derrida concludes, "a living image of life" or, better, "an image that steals life's point of view."[25]

However, the theft of life's point of view by the photographic image is still silent, inert, and imaginary, which is why photography makes the image a victim of a trap woven by time. Its limitation—in setting the objective of making us remember *what has been*, replacing the dying body with the fixed image—is the infinite mechanical reproduction of what has taken place only once and which can never be repeated. The photograph on the gravestone of the deceased is the infinite and static reproduction of an instant followed by nothing. Although it has appropriated the life of the dead, the photographic image will always represent them in the same way and, as a result, gives us the impression of being observed by a living person every time we go to the cemetery.

From TV to the Internet: A Gathering of Ghosts

With the invention of the phonograph, the radio, and especially TV, we move beyond the static analogy between the body and photography. The dead now have their voices and even their ability to move restored. This gives them a unique opportunity to "survive" death through sounds, images, and movement: repeating the same scenes for eternity. To the observer it's as if they've exchanged their mortal bodies for bodies that simulate them in the mobile repetitions of audiovisual images. When Kurt Cobain committed suicide in 1994, it wasn't enough to have his image captured in a photograph. Around the world television news shows featured his frenetic headbanging while the radio waves resounded with his punk vocals. For those who recorded it on their VHS or audio cassettes at the time, these broadcasts dedicated to Cobain—along with Nirvana's discography, articles about him in music magazines, and the few illegally distributed amateur bootleg recordings—were the mechanisms through which the singer was posthumously reconstituted.

Radio and television highlight "what can still exist," capitalizing on the confusion between real and alive, which Barthes talks about; leading us into a world where we can begin to imagine life without mortality. What that means is, for the first time, our human need to go beyond the concept of "You only live once" is met by creating millions of infinitely reproducible copies of moving, speaking images. The living presence of what these media are communicating is achieved through integrating the mechanism of repetition with that of television and radio recordings. As Maurizio Ferraris observes, recording fixes the subject to be communicated and is necessary for its codification and reception. Therefore, it has the power to defer and postpone, establishing and lending solidity and permanence to what seems changeable and unstable.[26]

Digital culture exponentially increases the communicative processes of recording and repetition, making the dead perpetually accessible to anyone with an internet connection. Digital recordings posted on social networks, YouTube, WordPress blogs, WhatsApp profiles, email servers, and cloud storage databases all preserve permanent, mobile traces of our activities, which are easy to reproduce and almost impossible to erase. This leaves us with the impression that all informational organisms, living or dead, can be found on the internet: indefinitely waiting, speaking, and participating in something.

The image's mobility is rendered even more autonomous because the informational organism lives in a narrative environment where individual and collective experience is constructed from layers of data and meaning, as well as hybridizations and interconnections. Historian Yuval Noah Harari interprets this type of experience as proof that we've moved on from humanism to what is known as "datism."

Humanism attributes personal, inner meaning to our experiences; giving credence to the internal, rational self in a way that encourages us to search for a personal, human-centered rationale for everything that happens. Dataists drastically rethink the role of finding meaning through individual soul searching, proposing that an experience's value depends solely on its being shared publicly. This is why they believe it's important to record and connect one's own experiences with the larger data flow, leaving it to the algorithms to determine their meaning and to recommend the best course of action.[27]

Moving past individual, inner experiences and merging with a global, interactive social vision of the human being is accompanied by the increasing self-sufficiency of our digital devices, which cooperate and interact with each other, often without our active or intentional participation. Simone Arcagni highlights this when, describing the post-cinematic landscape, he points out how the digital ecosphere (games, information, communication, and promotion) are in a state of constant interchange and overlap. Narratives shift in and out of a dizzying vortex and are autonomously generated and regenerated within an organic system. These are genuine transmedia strategies that correspond to a series of access possibilities generated by the viral and social character of the texts themselves.[28] On the one hand, this all supports the dataist theory of the connection of human experiences with larger data flows and the invasive role of algorithms, while on the other hand, it strongly reinforces the paradoxical situation of the dead, who are increasingly autonomous when compared to their survivors, in that they "steal" life from the image.

Following his suicide in May 2017, another grunge icon, Soundgarden's lead singer, Chris Cornell, continues to "live" in a very different way than Kurt Cobain did in the wake of his death. Cornell survives through hundreds (perhaps thousands) of live and studio video clips, interviews, amateur videos, photographs, photo montages, and various other audiovisual records, along with data and information. Thanks to the collaborative nature of the internet, the impressive amount of material related to Cornell, mostly on YouTube, continues to grow. And, it is randomly mixed in with the recorded experiences of the living. Even the singer's official website (http://www.chriscornell.com/) has become an interactive platform where his biographical pages are combined with those in which his family and fans post photographs, scans of paper letters, anecdotes, poetry, etc. All of this creates a huge, living archive of public and private memories—along with the possibility of confusing the past with the present.

Above all, digital technology makes Cornell's postmortem situation something that is achievable for anyone, famous or not. YouTube has an extensive archive of complete or fragmented videos in which we can watch the dead reciting, speaking, joking, and singing forever. This is what Ferraris calls an unlimited "gathering of ghosts"[29] which allows not only their still images to remain with us but also their voices, gestures, and movements. Indeed, there is no place on the internet that is *not* teeming with ghosts, easily mingling with the living through words, photographs, recordings, and videos. The past is always lurking just below the surface, conditioning the present.

And (Digital) Life Goes On…

The theoretical movement that, starting from the intimate link between death and the image, has led us from photography to digital culture allows us to understand the underlying reason why it is so commonplace for the living to mingle with communicable traces of the dead—and how difficult it can be to distinguish communication *at a distance* from communication *with the dead*. This movement is derived from the fundamental philosophical problem implicit in digital death: every time a person's life ends, its digital life continues to be active in a number of different formats and for an indefinite period of time.

On the one hand, our death always happens in an exceptional moment that literally constitutes a divergence relative to the preceding and following moments, in that it marks the end of our psychophysical identity. As Vladimir Jankélévitch said, this instant marks the beginning of eternity because it has no tomorrow and allows no turning back. And all living things are, as Georges Canguilhem observes, condemned to be "merely *viable*," and even then, lacking any guarantee of survival. For Canguilhem, living under this "death sentence" means that death and illness play a defining role in our lives and the lives of other living things; the inevitability of death renders it essential to every single organism's birth, growth, and development.[30]

On the other hand, in digital culture we keep living—as *informational organisms*—beyond that exceptional moment. We find ourselves in a position to effectively circumvent being condemned to mere viability and to "live" beyond that moment, which once marked the end of our present and the beginning of an eternal past. The date of someone's actual death does not coincide with their digital death. Once recorded within a digital environment, information, data, personal portraits, and moments lived will remain well beyond their death. Each individual is distributed, stored, and dispersed (in multiple representations, masks, and images) across a multitude of databases or in several virtual locations, often without their specific desire or consent.

At first, in the period immediately following their death, the digital body's reaction is similar to that of the physical body. Some bodily functions—like the growth of hair or nails on the corpse—remain active for a certain time period, giving the impression that the body hasn't quite accepted death. In the same way, the deceased's various accounts continue to receive mail, messages, tags, invitations, spam, phishing scams, and advertising as they usually would. Yet bodily functions, within days, do cease to operate. Not so with our digital body. Even as the data and information associated with the digital body are reduced once the news of a person's death has been made public, it valiantly lives on in its afterlife.

Insiders use the expression "posthumous interaction" to refer to the system of interaction with the digital data of the deceased. "Posthumous" refers only to those who are physically dead, not to their data, information, and digital objects, which continue to live an independent ghostly life. "For the dead man continues to move, and the corpse of the real never stops growing," Baudrillard writes.[31]

It's clear that the multiplication of psychophysical identities across multiple internet profiles and avatars offers a concrete alternative to philosopher Günther Anders's idea of "canned peaches," which he proposed (with regret) as a model for the human being, back in the 1950s. In contrast to the physical body, which is unique and irreplaceable, canned peaches are mass produced, following a standard prototype, distributed on a global scale, and therefore "immortal" in their own way.[32] But, like all mass-produced items, even canned peaches are destined to expire, just as Anders's idea (of which they are the concrete example) has become obsolete. When the idea underlying of a mass-produced object is no longer fashionable, and so doesn't ensure the manufacturer a predictable return on investment, the resulting products stop being manufactured and slowly disappear into thin air.

> "She will live forever in my memory!" *Live?* That is exactly what she won't do. You might as well think like the old Egyptians that you can keep the dead by embalming them. Will nothing persuade us that they are gone? What's left? A corpse, a memory, and ... a ghost. All mockeries or horrors.[33]

So wrote C. S. Lewis, in response to what he perceived to be an inane cliché about enduring lives after death. And indeed still today, in our digital culture, we continue to grapple with "what's left" of our lives online after we die. As Giovanni

Ziccardi reminds us, "Achieving oblivion—understood as the real and concrete possibility of erasing, or better yet permanently destroying, that information relative to your own past that is no longer either current or of public interest—is a radical and quintessential idea."[34] It is easier to de-index content on the internet, obscuring the results on the major search engines, than it is to try to permanently delete it.

I will now describe the different and specific characteristics of digital survival after biological death; therefore, the contemporary way of concretizing the paradox of the dead who becomes the incarnation of an absent presence. I should make it clear that we will be dealing with ghosts from here on out. First, with those ghosts that survive as digital replicas of human identities, reproducing their emotions, thoughts and beliefs, and thus defining the concept of "digital immortality."[35] But, second, with the ghosts manifested in the context of social networks—able to create new relationships between the dead and the living through photographs, videos, documents, stories, diaries, interviews, etc.—in which a mobile and living copy of everything the deceased saw, felt, and said remains. And finally, with those who create a digital memory, from which it seems impossible to free themselves; and with those who form innovative cemeteries and funerals, revealing themselves in practices that are unique and, at first glance, seemingly unorthodox. Thanks to these digital ghosts, we can easily mingle with communicable traces of the dead, while at the same time this very interaction makes it difficult for us, the living, to distinguish communication at a distance from communication with the dead.

1
Digital Immortality

Black Mirror: Be Right Back

On February 11, 2013, the first episode of the second season of *Black Mirror* was broadcast on the UK's Channel 4. It was entitled "Be Right Back." This popular British TV series has become a benchmark for fans of a dystopian vision of the future in that it wittily uses a dark, satirical tone in imagining how today's technology could develop in the future. This specific episode, which according to *Empire* film magazine includes one of the fifty greatest sci-fi moments in fiction, tells the story of a young English couple, Martha and Ash. They go shopping at the supermarket and sing Bee Gees songs in the car, smartphone always in hand: a married life like many others, until Ash dies in a traffic accident. And Martha, shattered by his loss, is both widowed and pregnant. After her initial reluctance, and in a moment of weakness, her best friend finally convinces her to install an app with a truly unique feature: it allows her to *keep* communicating with her dead boyfriend. It recreates the profile of the deceased with its specific personality traits and communicative style by reworking the words and images he shared on his social media profiles, chat threads, and private emails. The goal is easy to fathom: give the grieving person an effective tool to ease their immediate pain, which has been caused by the separation. First, Martha receives an email in her partner's name; then she clicks on the internal link to start a chat with him. "Is it really you?" she asks, sobbing. "No, it's the late Abraham Lincoln," Ash replies, mimicking the same ironic style he had when he was alive. She tells him that she's pregnant. "Wow. So I'll be a dad? I wish I was there with you now," the software responds. *I'll be a dad*.

Regardless of how surreal the situation is, a chat thread isn't enough for Martha. She wants to hear her boyfriend's voice again. Nothing could be easier. The software processes all of the videos that the couple has recorded over the years and artificially recreates Ash's voice. After a few minutes her phone rings. She answers and hears "his" voice. He makes a joke, pointing out that he is now *a voice without a mouth*. In the days that follow, Martha increasingly isolates herself from family and friends, leaving the house—*alone*—and talking on the telephone with Ash's mouthless voice. Seated in a field near a cliff, she takes a panoramic photo of the landscape so that the software can process the image and extract the necessary information about the area from the data it finds on a search engine. She tells Ash stories about their life together, remembering what a great guy he was. "You speak about me like I'm not here." On the day that she goes to the hospital to get her first ultrasound, she has a panic attack after she drops her phone. It's as if she has lost him all over again. When she is able to get in touch with him, he reassures her: he is not in the phone, *he is in a remote server in the cloud.*

The next step is even more extreme: the dead Ash can "come back" to his Martha by way of a blank, artificial body that has to be activated by following specific instructions. Now there is an artificial Ash, without a metabolism and no need to eat or sleep, moving around the house. He has no blood running through his veins, so he cannot be injured. He is aesthetically attractive and young: his image is taken from the original Ash's retouched Instagram photos, while his skin is smoother because it's based on a digital texture map of skin tissue. Every tiny detail is a 2D image. But, this artificial Ash lacks sensitivity and sexual appetite. Apparently, he never talked about sex in his private chats. However, this problem is easy to resolve: he learns how to perform from pornographic videos. Despite his porn star skills in bed, Martha slowly becomes aware of the false narrative that imprisons her. At a certain point she lashes out, "You're just a few ripples of you. There's no history to you. You're just a performance of stuff that he performed without thinking, and it's not enough." Ash ends up stored in the attic, but he is always ready to be reactivated if the weight of grief becomes unbearable. Exactly like a couple's old photo album full of memories that, after some time has passed, one of them feels the urge to leaf through.

Her, a Spike Jonze film released in 2013, has a storyline that is somewhat similar to that of "Be Right Back." It is not grief but separation from his ex-wife that pushes the lonely, melancholy Theodore Twombly to embark on a love affair with Samantha, the digital assistant that is part of an upgrade to his operating system "OS 1." Samantha is an artificial intelligence able to evolve through her own experience and through the thousands of personalities processed by her programmers, slowly adapting to the psychological and physical characteristics specific to each individual buyer. If Ash "became" an operating system that lives in the cloud, Samantha was "born" and lives out her life inside a computer. "I have no choice, that's my home," she confesses to Theodore, proud of not having a body. A physical body with circumscribed boundaries would objectively keep her from growing—limiting her and binding her to time and space—and in the end it would mean that she would have to die.

Record and Digitize: You'll Become Immortal!

At first glance, "Be Right Back" and *Her* seem to be nothing more than contemporary TV and film updates of classic science fiction narratives, which made writers like Isaac Asimov and Philip K. Dick famous, or of the visionary theories of Timothy Leary, best known for promoting the use of psychedelic drugs. Leary, in particular, offers an unusual introduction to his book *Design for Dying* with this explicit invitation, written in all caps: "IF YOU WANT TO IMMORTALIZE YOUR CONSCIOUSNESS, RECORD AND DIGITIZE."[1]

In truth, there is very little that is science fiction or visionary in these most recent films. In 2000, Gordon Bell and

Jim Gray, two famous Microsoft researchers, wrote a brief essay—much discussed among digital death scholars—in which they argue that digital immortality will be a reality within this century. And they are sure we could freely make use of it without thinking twice.[2]

What I mean first by the concept of "digital immortality" is the lasting fame achieved through the preservation and transmission of ideas. This is just like "ordinary" mortality. Aristotle, Shakespeare, Mozart, and Rembrandt are dead (as individual human beings) but their ideas and creations have become immortal, recorded and passed down to the present day. However, I am also talking about limitless, active experiences and learning that can be achieved through the technological tools that we currently have available.

The first kind of immortality is a one-way street. It allows us to communicate with the future through what we have produced during our lifetimes. The second kind of immortality runs both ways. It allows us to communicate with the future through what we have produced during our lifetimes, *and* it also offers us the opportunity to *continue* to learn and evolve. We are not content with what we have been during our lifetimes and with what we have bequeathed to future generations: artworks, books, scientific discoveries, or even just kindness and good manners. We would prefer to concretize Woody Allen's famous comment, often cited in transhumanist studies: "I don't want to become immortal through my work. I want to become immortal through not dying."

According to the two Microsoft researchers, in order to achieve this two-way immortality we need to convert part of ourselves into information and data, which will be recorded and digitized using modern media. In other words: RECORD AND DIGITIZE. With that goal in mind, since the end of the last century Bell has been working to record every single thing that is happening in his life, even to the point of keeping prescriptions, receipts, and PDF files of every web page he has visited. He has a SenseCam around his neck at all times. Invented by Microsoft, this particular camera automatically takes a photograph every time it senses any change in its surroundings. In this way it takes advantage of the informational nature of humans and the integration between our online and off-line worlds; worlds that are marked by our existence, validating Harari's thesis concerning the historical transition from humanism to what he calls *datism*. Bell, disputing the theory proposed by Viktor Mayer-Schönberger in his book *Delete: The Virtue of Forgetting in the Digital Age* (2009)—according to which remembering all of the sensory stimuli that bombard us would overload human memory and its capacity to store information—holds that, on the contrary, forgetting is a human flaw. Therefore, it is necessary to record everything while waiting for a perfect digital copy of yourself to be created, through which you can finally achieve immortality.[3]

He is not the only one who thinks so. Eighteen euros a month for batteries is what Muscovite Alexey Turchin says he spends to follow Bell and Gray's plan. Since 2015, after failing to create a supercomputer that would bring a deceased friend back to life, he has been recording all his daily experiences, without exception, uploading them to the cloud and making backups on Blu-ray discs, which he claims will last a thousand years. Together with a colleague, Turchin has launched a company known as Digital Immortality Now, where he brings his experiments together. His aim is to supply inexpensive tools for preserving personal information that would allow the puzzle of an individual identity to be reconstructed from pieces of data.

In the 1970s, Erkki Kurenniemi—a Finnish pioneer in the fields of multimedia art, electronic music, and industrial robotics, as well as one of the founders of Helsinki University's Musicology Department—argued that algorithms would soon become our descendants. He also argued that computers and humans would be integrated to create a kind of "superhuman." With that in mind, he created an archive that documented his entire life, a kind of interactive database, or digital autobiography, to be preserved until July 10, 2048, the year in which—according to his calculations—a computer would be able to reactivate his existence by way of a virtual avatar. Kurenniemi died in 2017 and now his digital autobiography— including video recordings, photographs, writings, etc.—has been displayed in the context of several art exhibits and is held at Kiasma, Helsinki's contemporary art museum. It was used to create Mika Taanila's documentary *The Future Is Not What It Used to Be*. Despite all of his efforts, in the end Kurenniemi has only achieved one-way digital immortality.

Many people believe that these experiments are either really creepy or the bizarre results of technological fanaticism on the part of some computer geek who doesn't clearly understand the public spaces in which we live. In reality, technological innovations and inventions that seek to achieve digital immortality are on the increase. The common goal is to *ensure the survival of one's own identity*, as a kind of digital ghost, *after the actual death of the person who has "embodied" it during their lifetime*. This would enable people to achieve the two-way immortality that Bell talks about and that we see represented in *Black Mirror*: communicating with the future while continuing to learn and evolve. The starting point is the paradoxical status of the dead: the dialectic between presence and absence that, if technologically manipulated, can also represent the starting point from which to actively reconstruct that entity in a way that extends beyond the static photographic image. The image that, until recently, has been the primary repository of its existence.

In the following pages I will first describe a few projects that, inspired by the adventures of Martha and Ash, are now being implemented in a concrete way. Just a few short years ago, projects like this seemed far-fetched and unattainable. These projects allow the continuation of digital life beyond the confines of physical death. After that, I will analyze those projects from a philosophical perspective, clearly presenting both sides of the coin: the opportunities and the inherent risks.

Chatting with the Dead: Eugenia Kuyda and James Vlahos

On November 28, 2015, a young Belarusian man died when he was run down by a car in Moscow. His name was Roman

Mazurenko and, barely into his thirties, he was already known in the city's cultural and artistic circles for his ability to organize public events. The founder of Stampsy, a tool for creating digital magazines, Roman was interested in scientific progress, especially in the theory of "technological singularity." This theory doesn't have a single explanation. Kevin Kelly, editor and co-founder of *Wired* magazine, describes the technological singularity as that fateful moment in history when the changes that have happened over millions of years will be superseded by the change that will take place in the next five minutes. Raymond Kurzweil, an American inventor and computer scientist, defines it slightly differently as the future time when technological change will be so rapid and have such a radical sociocultural impact that human life will be irreversibly changed. Generally, the technological singularity indicates a fast-approaching period in our history when the human mind will be able to augment its intelligence exponentially, establishing a fruitful partnership between physics and technology. Once this milestone has been reached, humans will be their brain, which is then uploaded to an electronic device, thus avoiding the organic degradation of the body. This copy could itself be copied multiple times, allowing humanity to achieve an unprecedented cognitive expansion that would be supported by robotic bodies.[4]

In addition to his specific interest in the technological singularity, Roman had an unusual curiosity about death and immortality. He had even designed, albeit unsuccessfully, a cemetery where the dead would have been buried in biodegradable capsules that would have fertilized trees as they decomposed, creating a forest. Each tree would have been equipped with an individual digital code associated with the deceased so that their relatives would have been able to read their basic biographical information.

In the days following his death, Roman's friend Eugenia Kuyda reread some private messages that she had exchanged with him starting in 2008, the year they met. She also thought back to his interest in the link between death, ecology, and digital technology. Her friend hadn't been very interested in social networks and had rarely used Facebook, Twitter, and Instagram. What he did have was a characteristically distinctive way of communicating in his written messages, influenced by his mild dyslexia and idiosyncratic phrases. In conversations with friends, he often stressed his astonishment at death's remoteness from people's everyday lives, lives that were increasingly lived online. Eugenia, who during the previous year had been working on a startup project called Luka, which could emulate human dialogue, decided to modify it after she saw "Be Right Back."

The pain caused by her friend's death drove her to wonder whether or not it made sense for each of us to remain nothing more than a random puzzle of lifeless, written words, strewn about in some antiquated electronic archive. So she decided to make Luka a functional version of the software imagined by the creators of *Black Mirror*: a tool that would allow her to communicate with Roman's "digital ghost." Eugenia asked Roman's friends and relatives to send her the written messages they had received from him. She ended up with several thousands of messages from which she excluded content that was too personal. With the help of some friends who were computer scientists, she created a bot that could mimic human language and make it possible to communicate with Roman. Joseph Weizenbaum's program Eliza served as a benchmark for Eugenia's project. Eliza had been created in 1966 and was the first software able to interact in a way that was indistinguishable from human interaction, thus passing the Turing test.

The chat messages that can be read on websites like The Verge, where Roman's story is described in meticulous detail, closely resemble the written dialogues between Martha and Ash. "How are you there?" asks a friend. "I'm OK. A little down. I hope you aren't doing anything interesting without me," Roman responds. His friend replies that they all miss him. Another acquaintance asks him if God and the soul exist. Having probably indicated his atheism in chats while he was alive, he says no. "Only sadness."

Not content with Luka, Eugenia also designed a chatbot called Replika (https://replika.ai/). A cross between a diary and a personal assistant, Replika asks a series of questions— investigating and learning about each person—and eventually learns to mimic their communication style. The goal is to get closer to creating a digital avatar that would be able to reproduce us and replace us once we're dead, but also one that is able to create "friendships" with humans. Since the second half of 2017, over two million people have downloaded Replika onto their mobile devices. Eugenia continues to develop the bot's *emotional* responsiveness so that it will become even more of a "virtual friend" that users can confide in. In other words, Replika is the real-life version of Samantha from the movie *Her*: a chatbot that can empathize with a human by using a type of deep learning, called *sequence-to-sequence*, which learns to think and speak like a human by processing transcripts of conversations they've had during their lifetimes.[5]

Luka and Replika are not the only inventions designed to give a voice to the digital ghosts of the deceased. James Vlahos, an American journalist who has been an AI enthusiast since childhood, recently created what he calls a "Dadbot." It all started on April 24, 2016, when his father John was diagnosed with lung cancer. Born in 1936 and raised in California by Greek immigrant parents, John Vlahos was a successful lawyer, an amateur thespian (some of the productions he was in were even televised), and a college football fan. He was also gifted with a strong sense of irony, wit, and charm. Upon learning of his father's illness, his son James initially just wanted him to tell his father's life story. He recoded all of their conversations with the idea of writing a commemorative book after John's death. After twelve sessions, each an hour and a half, he found himself with 91,970 words. The printed transcripts filled around 203 pages. They contained a number of memories, songs, and anecdotes and touched on John's marriage, the high points of his career, and all of his passionate interests. All of this material, in addition to being transcribed, is also archived in MP3 files on James's computer.

One day James came across an online article describing a project carried out by two Google researchers. It involved entering around twenty-six million lines of movie dialog into a neural network in order to build a chatbot that could interact with humans. Having achieved their objective, the two researchers started asking their chatbot a series of philosophical questions including one about the purpose of life. The response was "To live forever." A lightbulb went off in James's head and he decided to use the recordings of his father to create something other than a commemorative book. He remembered having written an article that discussed Pull-String (previously known as ToyTalk), a program designed to create conversations with fictional characters. PullString helped design, among others, the Hello Barbie Hologram, a box that makes it possible to project a three-dimensional animation of the famous doll, Barbie. Like Apple's Siri, the Hello Barbie Hologram responds to users' voice commands and her narrative potential grows through constant interaction.

The journalist used PullString to reorganize the MP3 recordings of his father, which he had archived on his computer. He also used it to create his Dadbot, software that works on his smartphone and simulates a written conversation with John, based on the processing of almost a hundred thousand recorded words. Since John's death, James still chats with him, softening the blow of his loss. During public presentations of the Dadbot, he has said that his son also writes messages to his grandfather's digital ghost sometimes and receives replies. The tone of the conversations reflects the personality of the deceased: "Where are you now?" asks James. "As a bot I suppose I exist somewhere on a computer server in San Francisco. And also, I suppose, in the minds of people who chat with me." Just like Ash, who is living in the cloud, and Samantha, inside a computer.[6]

A few years ago, Type O Negative, a goth metal band from Brooklyn, sang "Halloween in Heaven," a song that imagines how deceased rock musicians—like Jimi Hendrix and John Lennon—would be happily celebrating this iconic American holiday with rivers of Jack Daniels on a cloud in heaven. These days, such a party could still happen on a cloud—albeit one that exists on a hard drive.

Social Networks for the Dead: Eterni.me and Eter9

In the wake of Eugenia Kuyda and James Vlahos's projects came Eterni.me (http://eterni.me/), a startup conceived by the Romanian programmer Marius Ursache and developed as part of the MIT Entrepreneurship Development Program. The official website's homepage greets visitors with a question posed in large, bold type: "Who wants to live forever?" This is followed by a promise to preserve each user's most important thoughts, stories, and memories for eternity. The theoretical starting point of Eterni.me is the bitter realization that, as time moves forward from the moment of an individual's death, that person is doomed to disappear, despite photographs, videos, and letters or diaries left to family and friends. This service—still in the beta testing phase so you can still sign up free of charge—doesn't just want to create a static treasure trove of memories. If anything, it wants to generate a *living*, digital copy of subjective identity that is able to maintain the functionality of all the qualities and abilities that characterized individual users during their lifetimes, even after death.

When Eterni.me becomes active, we will be invited to provide its database with information, primarily related to our personal passions and habits shared on the internet. We will have to give the software our "digital objects": vacation snapshots, selfies, videos we love or ones that show us with our friends, love letters written over the years, political opinions, etc. In other words, everything that we've ever published on our social networks or blogs and our emails—everything that best defines our own *unique* personalities. The software will extract from this "digital life" the necessary user data, which it will then analyze, looking for unique relationships and patterns. The scope of this project is to create a digital ghost that represents what we have been, creating a virtual identity able to interact with our loved ones and, therefore, replace us, reflecting and preserving both our strengths and our weaknesses. For example, if a person is a big fan of hard rock, and posted multiple video clips of songs from groups like Black Sabbath on their Facebook page, it's very likely that once they are dead, their Eterni.me profile will continue to post music videos of the band. Or, alternatively, that person's digital ghost might "talk about" the discography of the British group with their living friends, arguing that the band's recent song "Live Forever" doesn't quite reach the heights of classics such as "Killing Yourself to Live."

The service will use a 3D digital avatar, developed by researchers at MIT, capable of emulating the personality of the subject, providing content to those friends and family members that are included on an approved list. The digital heritage obtained will be available to the deceased's descendants to provide them with, first, all of the useful information about that person's habits and interests and, second, an opportunity to communicate with their immortal, virtual twin.

The website's presentation highlights the opportunity to eternally preserve our personal memories for our children, grandchildren, and descendants. This storehouse of memories, taken as a whole, is conceived not so much as a digital legacy, but rather as a kind of *individual multimedia library*. Instead of putting books in this library, users can deposit interactive histories of current and future generations. Over 40,000 people have already signed up, and this number is expected to increase over the coming years. Scrolling down the homepage, you'll find the phrase "Become Virtually Immortal." As the service develops, our alter egos will become—as Ursache intends—increasingly accurate, and above all similar to what we would like to have been and, perhaps, what we never were.

A similar service Eter9 (https://www.eter9.com/auth /login) is already partially active (the name comes from a combination of "Eternity" and "Cloud 9"). The brainchild of Portuguese programmer Henrique Jorge, it turns out to be a very unusual social network. In setting up a newsfeed similar to that of Facebook, Eter9 uses data mining resources to produce its core content. The concept is to create an automated post generator that can also publish videos and images, even when users are off-line.

Eter9 works like this: each user registers, choosing a username and password, and then enters a virtual environment almost identical to that of Facebook. What you'll find first is the "Bridge" with glacial colors and a futuristic background. On the Bridge, you can write posts and share all kinds of videos and links. You can make friends with other users, with whom you interact like you do on Facebook: commenting on each other's posted content and clicking on a "smile" button that takes the place of Facebook's iconic like button.

The first unusual feature that you'll encounter is that, instead of the post prompt: "What's on your mind?" you'll see the following: "Think something to eternity." And in fact, each user is able to "eternalize" their shared content within specific categories, which range from music to technology, science, sports, movies, and travel. An explanation of the "eternalize" option is found in the page adjacent to the Bridge called the "Cortex." On the same day you register on Eter9, your virtual alter ego is born in the Cortex. This entity is known as your "Counterpart." The goal of this virtual alter ego is first and foremost to understand the human whom it is meant to imitate by analyzing what that individual published on the Bridge, including interactions with other users. Its second job is to replace and replicate that user when they are off-line and (yes!) even when that person is dead. Of course that is once the Counterpart has learned about the user's behavior and way of interacting. My

Counterpart is named d4v1d3 s1570 and was born on April 20, 2017.

To all intents and purposes, the Counterpart is responsible for the user's eternal life, as well as for the equally eternal ghost that will take the user's place as their heir, annulling the distance between off-line and online. Clearly, the more you interact in the Eter9 environment, the more your Counterpart learns, enhancing its qualities. According to Jorge, interacting with other users or other virtual Counterparts also increases the probability of better emulation. Each individual can decide what level of autonomy to give their Counterpart, assigning a percentage from 0 to 100 percent. If you choose 100 percent, then your Counterpart will be very active, frequently sharing thoughts and links whenever you are off-line. However, if you choose 0 percent then Eter9 works exactly like any other social network. It's also possible to decide on the "lifespan" of your Counterpart, preparing a digital will through an electronic service called Perpetu.

In order to help those who are new to the network learn the basics of how the Eter9 platform functions (such as how to use the Bridge and initiate private chats), a bot, ELiZA NiNE, is available to explain how everything works. In addition to ELiZA NiNE, several other forms of artificial intelligence are available. Known as Niners, they interact both with humans and among themselves. The most unusual and disturbing aspect of Jorge's invention is how difficult it is to distinguish between the human users and the artificial ones. In theory, each one of us could log on to Eter9 and quibble about politics, musical tastes, and movies with humans and nonhumans alike, without ever noticing the difference. It even begs the question of whether or not bots can also be duped by fake news. It won't be long before posting information will be automatic, with no real need for flesh and blood people. For now, Eter9 is a social network like any other. The Counterparts have not truly come to life yet, but they are slowly starting to.

LivesOn, another project along these same lines, has failed. Developed by the British company Mean Fighting Machine, LivesOn was very similar to Eter9, although more like Twitter than Facebook. That said, the goal was the same: those who created a free account on the LivesOn platform allowed this social network access to their Twitter content. LivesOn would then carefully research the kinds of tweets and retweets a user posted, as well as their network of contacts, with the goal of continuing to author similar tweets after the user's death. The company slogan was "When your heart stops beating, you'll keep tweeting." LivesOn is still online, but now its focus is on helping clients define their lifestyle, offering information on vacation spots, entertainment, sports, and so forth.

Avatars and Holograms: LifeNaut, ForeverIdentity, and "DIO Returns"

Somewhat similar to the projects previously described, LifeNaut (https://www.lifenaut.com/) is working on creating digital clones of humans, which will be able to think and act like us or, even instead of us. This web-based research project is linked to the Terasem Movement Foundation, an American organization that investigates strategies for extending human life. It supports educational programs and scientific research in the areas of cryogenics, biotechnology, and cyberconsciousness. Its philosophical manifesto is the book entitled *The Day You Discard Your Body* by Marshall Brain (yes, that is his real name), computer programmer and founder of HowStuffWorks as well as the author of several essays relevant to transhumanist thought. The book's polemical target is the human body, initially explored—a bit naively—through the science fiction narratives of writers such as William Gibson and Aldous Huxley. According to Brain, giving up one's biological body means achieving a level of freedom and longevity that is unimaginable today. The final line of chapter 14 could serve as a slogan: "Discarding your body will be the smart, logical and obvious thing to do."[7] Interestingly enough, this slogan was taken up by Zoltan Istvan who was a candidate in the 2016 U.S. presidential election. This transhumanist philosopher traveled around the country—together with a hippie, a robot named Jethro, and Russian man carrying the frozen brain of his dead mother—in a coffin-shaped bus (the Immortality Bus), promising voters eternal life. Looking at his poor results, it appears that he didn't convince many. However, Istvan believed in himself and decided to run again, this time for governor of California—an election in which he garnered 0.2 percent of the vote.

Today, LifeNaut makes it possible to create both a Mind-File and a BioFile. The MindFile is a database that functions as a type of electronic backup of a person's personality. It is a virtual space where the user can organize and preserve information in digital format—photographs, videos, personal documents, etc.—with the goal of creating a meaningful and substantial portrait of the individual. To make this portrait mobile and "living," each user needs to respond to around five hundred questions about their personality. The responses are then processed in order to recreate an exact psychological profile of each user. The final result should be an electronically animated avatar that uses a voice synthesizer to describe some key events from the user's life. This avatar will connect with other people—living *and* dead—who are interested in exploring the future of technology and enhancing quality of life. Equipped with the user's facial features, after an individual's death, these avatars will interact primarily with the surviving relatives and embody the first principle of digital immortality: what matters is the fullness of your mental self, which can and must be transferred to a technological body that will enhance and add value to it.

The second aspect of the project is the BioFile. Once a request has been made, the user receives a type of mouthwash and a collection tube. They gargle with it, spit it into the collection tube, and then send it back to LifeNaut. At LifeNaut, DNA is extracted from the sample and cryogenically frozen so that it will be possible to clone that individual as soon as it becomes scientifically possible. The people who invented the BioFile make Don DeLillo, who wrote the visionary novel *Zero K* (2016) on the theme of cryogenics, look like an amateur.

LifeNaut's official ambassador is Bina48. Like Eter9's ELiZA NiNE, Bina48 is a robot created using a combination of transcriptions of video interviews, facial recognition, AI, and other resources. Her skin is made of *frubber*, a rubbery material that makes it possible for her to smile, frown, and make other expressions that allow her resemble a human in every way. Her features echo those of Bina Aspen, co-founder of the Terasem Movement Foundation. Bina48 has her own Facebook page (https://www.facebook.com/iambina48) and performs the fundamental task of providing the necessary support to help users to create a personal avatar. She is so evolved that in 2017 she even attended (and successfully passed) a class on the philosophy of love at California's Notre Dame de Namur University where she also discussed personal relationships with the other students.

The transition from robots like Bina48 to genuine holograms is a task that has been undertaken by FOREVER Identity (http://www.foreveridentity.com/), invented by three Italian researchers: Fabrizio Gramuglio, Giorgio Manfredi, and Tamara Zanella. They were inspired by steampunk, transhumanism, and Alexander Zinoviev's book *The Global Humant Hill* (1997). In addition to providing digital memory preservation services, FOREVER Identity is working on creating 3D holograms of historical figures and artists, reproducing their personalities, behaviors, physical traits, voices, and posture. Uniquely, the hologram will also be able to express emotions through a simulation of facial expressions and body language, and it will be able to describe its work and personal experiences, interacting with human users and reproducing a variety of intellectual, ethical, and moral characteristics. The goal is to provide museums, schools, and universities with a tool that will be useful for quickly and effectively disseminating cultural content.

With FOREVER Identity, in the tradition of Eter9's Counterparts and LifeNaut's avatars, we are now dealing with a hologram whose creation is currently a much-debated topic in scientific and technological circles. More than just a device used in movies and music, the use of holograms is now an established fact, with all of the polemics that entails.

Paul Walker, the American actor famous for his portrayal of Brian O'Conner in the *Fast and Furious* movie franchise, died in a car accident on November 30, 2013. He was forty years old and had finished filming 65 percent of the scenes for what was to be the seventh film in the well-known action series, *Furious 7* (2015). In order to complete the final part of the film, and not lose millions in financing, Universal Pictures managed to superimpose a 3D model of the deceased actor's face over those of his living brothers, Caleb and Cody Walker, who were serving as stand-ins. Finally, they used a third actor, John Brotherton, to voice some of Paul's lines. In order to do this, Universal called in Peter Jackson's company, Weta Digital, which had also done similar work for the movie *Gladiator* (2000) following the death of Oliver Reed. This story also brings to mind Alex Proyas's *The Crow* (1994), where the final scenes were completed using a digitally composite version of Brandon Lee's face and stunt doubles following the actor's tragic death during the last days of filming.

In the music world the focus of public attention has been on Ronnie James Dio, the iconic front man for heavy metal groups such as Elf, Rainbow, Black Sabbath, and Dio. Following the musician's death from stomach cancer in 2010, his hologram—created by Eyellusion (http://eyellusionlive.com)—started a world tour in 2017 with the evocative title "DIO Returns." The hologram is expected to continue touring in the future. The live performance involves playing back recordings of the singer's past performance of a song with the instrumental accompaniment of a living band. In 2019, an updated version of Dio's hologram was created, which includes particular attention to physical details (for example, eyebrows). According to his widow, Wendy Dio, the Italian American singer was someone who appreciated experimentation and would have consented to this kind of project. The stage is organized so that there is a kind of pedestal, at center stage, where Dio is projected going through his typical performance for every song. The tour has already been sold out in many venues around the world. "Long Live Rock 'n' Roll" was one of his classics, and if rock and roll can enjoy a long life, why shouldn't it keep going and live forever?

After their experience with "DIO Returns," Eyellusion is now working on a hologram of the American composer and guitarist Frank Zappa, who died in 1993 and was known for his musical experimentation. The goal is to make it possible for those who were too young to have seen a Frank Zappa concert while he was alive, to enjoy the extraordinary experiences of his live concerts that left their indelible mark on the 1960s and 1970s. To date holograms have been used to reproduce Prince and Michael Jackson as well as other famous musicians.

Beyond the world of movies and music, an increasing number of companies and startups are imagining a world populated by both humans and holograms. A representative example is Magic Leap (https://www.magicleap.com/), which is working on inserting virtual images in a user's field of vision. Among the more interesting companies is New Zealand's 8i (https://8i.com), which has been working in Los Angeles and San Francisco since 2014. The company is working on creating 3D holograms of humans that have lifelike volume and can be projected into the same environment with flesh-and-blood people. By focusing on the realistic quality of the images, 8i aims to achieve human immortality through holographic representations. An example might be taking a photograph of a deceased relative and projecting a volumetric image onto it so that it would give the impression of being alive. Another example is that of the Shoah Foundation in Los Angeles, which created the New Dimensions in Testimony project (2012–present) in collaboration with the University of Southern California's Institute for Creative Technologies (ICT). This involved the creation of a hologram that portrays a very realistic likeness of holocaust survivor Pinchas Gutter; it moves naturally as it talks to high school students about the atrocities suffered by Jews in the Nazi concentration camps.

These latest inventions make it possible for us to envision a near future, certainly influenced by augmented reality, that will involve interactions not only with chatbots and

Counterparts but also with holograms of ordinary people—above all, with the dead. The recent film *Marjorie Prime* (2017), directed by Michael Almereyda and based on Jordan Harrison's 2015 Pulitzer Prize–nominated play of the same name, deals with this concept of evolving digital immortality. Set in the very near future, the film tells the story of Marjorie, an eighty-six-year-old woman who is widowed when her husband Walter dies. Her daughter, to help her mother cope with his loss, allows her to use a program that reproduces Walter, as a hologram, sitting on the living room sofa. This digital ghost appears to the woman as she wanted to remember her husband, so he looks like a younger version of himself. The holographic reproduction increasingly takes on the behavioral characteristics of her deceased husband as both Marjorie and other relatives tell him about his life. His job is to converse with the old woman, remembering their life together, in order to help ameliorate Marjorie's Alzheimer's symptoms as well as ease her suffering. In the end, Walter is not the only hologram in this story: others enter the scene as the family is reduced over time by the deaths of other members.

In providing another possible interpretation of future digital immortality, this film focuses on how giving precedence to memories and recorded evidence from the characters' actual lives changes how their holographic selves evolve. No one is who they have been, and no one will be who they are now: each digital ghost is only able to learn how to imitate the departed through the stories told by their relatives. These recollections are full of omissions, some voluntary as when a given memory evokes a painful event. So the life of a digital ghost is the sum of the various ways in which the relatives and friends of the deceased remember them. A marriage proposal that happened in an ordinary hotel room while watching *My Best Friend's Wedding* on TV can be transformed into a romantic declaration of love after going to see *Casablanca* at the cinema. In this way reality becomes just a question of imaginative storytelling and retelling. A painful past experience disappears in this ghostly reworking of the narrative, as if it had never occurred.

In 2013, *Black Mirror's* "Be Right Back" episode and the movie *Her* both foreshadowed a world in which it is possible to text, talk, and even make love with an artificial replica of the deceased. Many of the ideas imagined and developed in the writing of these works have become realistic possibilities that will be achievable within a few short years. *Marjorie Prime* even imagined a future world without human beings. A world inhabited solely by digital ghosts, sitting and talking in the living room in which they were programmed, interacting based on the more or less authentic stories with which they had been inculcated. If this science fiction also turns out to be possible, will the world become home to (more or less accurate) ghostly projections of what we were purely based on subjective and unreliable "memory"? And will these entities come to be valued more than the living, on whom such memories are based?

The kind of digital immortality that is the aim of these projects (evidenced both in sci-fi movies and high-tech firms) takes shape according to these three specific approaches—chatbots, Counterparts, and holograms—taking advantage of the dissociation between digital life and biological life. These technological inventions seem inspired by the challenge that death presents; they are the result of our desire to create a digital "cure" for death and the pain and suffering caused by the loss of someone you love. The lesson that clearly emerges from the narrative of *Black Mirror*'s "Be Right Back" episode, as well as all of the other projects mentioned in this chapter, is that often our interest in digital afterlives hinges on digital immortality not so much as an end in itself—although it does stimulate the imagination of technophiles—but rather as a means of providing succor to grieving loved ones.

The End of Every Possible World

> The death of another, especially if we love them, is not the declaration of an absence, a disappearance, the end of *this or that life*, that is to say the possibility of a world (always unique) to appear to a living person. Death declares *the end of the world in its totality* each time, the end of every possible world, and *each time the end of the world as a unique totality and therefore irreplaceable and therefore infinite*. ... The end of the world itself, of the only existing world, every time. Individually. Irreversibly. For the other, and oddly even for those who survive for the moment and endure the impossible experience. This is what the "world" can mean. And this meaning is conferred on it only by that which is known as "death."[8]

As Derrida argues, every time someone we loved dies, the whole world ends—or seems to. Habits, customs, rituals, and languages that made up the world, the only possible world as far as we were aware, vanish together with the lives of those who have died. Not only do the experiences and intimacies end, that particular way of speaking and interacting also ceases to exist, the specific meaning of which is totally encompassed within the exclusive and unrepeatable relationship with the person who is no longer alive. Every Sunday at lunchtime, my girlfriend and I buy ten pastries that we divide equally as a way of having a small weekly celebration. If one of us dies, this ritual will also die, because it is an integral part of a world—our world—that will have come to an end. Doing the same thing with another person would never have that same, unique meaning; it would lack everything that characterized and sustained our specific ritual. Just think of the simplest aspects of that ritual: how each of us takes a pastry out of the package or chooses which one to eat first. C. S. Lewis argues that, if salt were forbidden, one wouldn't notice the lack of it more in one food than in another, but the act of eating itself would be different. In the same way, the act of living is radically different when a loved one dies.[9] *This is what the word "world" can mean*: a meaning that is contained within the irreplaceable gestures of a relationship between two people, whether they are friends, lovers, or relatives, and that is conferred by what we define as "death."

The awareness of the end of every possible world and of the role the deceased played in defining the borders of this unique and irrevocably lost world, is that which—according to Maurice Merleau-Ponty—likens the bond between the bereaved and the departed to the relationship between a person suffering from anosognosia (an inability or refusal to recognize a clinically evident disorder, such as paralysis) and their paralyzed limb:

> We do not understand the absence or death of a friend until the time comes when we expect a reply from him and when we realize that we shall never again receive one; so at first we avoid asking in order not to have to notice this silence; we turn aside from those areas of our life in which we might meet this nothingness, but this very fact necessitates that we intuit them. In the same way the anosognosic leaves his paralyzed arm out of account in order not to have to feel his handicap, but this means that he has a preconscious knowledge of it.[10]

In order not to perceive this silence, the first thing we do is avoid asking any questions. When the death of a loved one marks the end of every possible world, we know that there will no longer be answers to them. Therefore, we escape from the silence of expectation and absence by not asking questions, despite the fact that we know this emptiness exists, in the same way that the anosognosic denies a disabled limb, knowing full well that it exists and is still part of them. And when (perhaps even without wanting to) we once again expect a response, we remain poised between our longing to see the face of our beloved once again and the clear awareness that this longing is doomed to failure.

We find ourselves in this type of situation when we are rearranging the photographs of a person who has died. In his book *Camera Lucida: Reflections on Photography*, Roland Barthes gives an excellent description of this sense of suspension when he is dealing with photographs of his deceased mother. He recognizes her in the separate details of a photograph—a region of her face, the movement of her arms, or the relationship between her nose and her forehead—which at the same time emphasizes how no single photograph captures her essence and identity. The more these images are partially true the more they are—at the same time—totally *un*true. The partial and fragmented borders that memory places at the end of every possible world do nothing more than emphasize this end, highlighting it. "It was not she, and yet it was no one else. I would have recognized her among thousands of other women, yet I did not 'find' her," observes Barthes,[11] to the extent that the limited and fragmentary nature of this memory makes the photograph comparable to a dream. While he is dreaming of his dead mother, he knows that it is her, but at the same time he realizes that it isn't her. There is always something misplaced or excessive that alters her features, making her perpetually out of place. "And confronted with the photograph, as in the dream, it is the same effort, the same Sisyphean labor: to reascend, straining toward the essence, to climb back down without having seen it, and to begin all over again."[12] In other words, the mourning process is limited. It can erase the immediate emotions associated with loss, but never the pain. Everything remains immobile, since through death we lose not an image but an entire world, therefore something irreplaceable. "I could live without the Mother (as we all do, sooner or later); but what life remained would be absolutely and entirely *unqualifiable* (without quality)."[13]

The chatbots invented by Eugenia Kuyda and James Vlahos, just like the Counterparts created in Eter9 and the digital copies of Eterni.me, are attempts to save the living from
the end of every possible world, hanging on to the bond that
death has dissolved. They are trying to succeed where photography and dreams fail. Digital immortality is designed,
as I mentioned before, from the perspective of those who
remain, not of those who have died. As Luigi Pirandello
argued, "Those who think they are alive also think that they
are crying for their dead. Instead, they are crying for one of
their own deaths, one of their own realities, which no longer
exists in the hearts of those who have died."[14] In keeping up
an active interaction with the dead, the chatbots appear to
keep us concentrated on "our" death, which is the death of
our ties to the other as *we* have experienced them, from our
exclusive point of view, up to the point of separation. It has
to do with that reality, which is no longer bound up with
the emotions of those who have left us behind. The chatbots
want to make it possible for *us* to still receive replies during that moment of suspension in which we are waiting for
an answer, or at least when we feel the need, softening the
pain brought on by the irreversibility of time and filling the
infinite space in between "before" and "after." As Martine
Rothblatt points out, what amazes us about the current technological possibilities, and the sophisticated forms of artificial intelligence that are emerging, is that they give us hope
that we can continue relationships that are objectively over.
Reminiscing with those who are no longer with us, talking
to them about our hopes and dreams, sharing the joys of

special celebrations: all of this happens after that person's physical body has turned to dust.[15]

To that end, the chatbots disrupt the coping mechanism of conscious or preconscious dissimulation, referenced by Merleau-Ponty, with a process of active *simulation*. This takes us from the question that has been intentionally avoided, in order to avoid remembering that there will not be an answer, to a death negated, even if we know perfectly well that it actually happened. The digital ghosts of Roman Mazurenko and of James Vlahos's father, like the Counterparts that replace us in Eter9, put us in the position of feigning possession of that which we no longer possess, relying as much on our full awareness of the loss as on our simultaneous desire to deny it. These beings pretend to hold open the door to a world that death has closed by effectively utilizing the continued existence of digital objects. Their fictional narrative is consistent with our own experience of a digital existence that is dissociated from our biological one, with our habit of delegating our stories and memories to artificial agents, with our fear of dead bodies, and thus with the informational nature that is the defining characteristic of our current relationship with the internet. All of this allows today's digital ghosts to be more alive than ever.

Can You Keep the Door Open to a World Forever Closed?

To better understand the mechanism of the fictional narrative the digital ghosts have set in motion, it's useful to keep in mind the works of Merleau-Ponty regarding the experience of dialogue. "As the parts of my body together comprise a system, so my body and the other's are one whole, two sides of one and the same phenomenon, and the anonymous existence of which my body is the ever-renewed trace henceforth inhabits both bodies simultaneously."[16] The experience of dialogue is the most direct proof of this mechanism because it produces *common ground* between the two participants. Their thoughts and their words, stimulated by the ongoing discussion, form a *unique fabric* that neither can claim as an autonomous creation. According to the French phenomenologist, while they are engaged in dialogue, the participants become "collaborators for each other in consummate reciprocity." Therefore, the two perspectives that they embody are integrated and coexist in a single, unique world. In other words, dialogue frees them from themselves. In turn, the thoughts expressed are emancipated from the individual who voices them, taking on an autonomous form according to the direction the dialogue takes. Each objection that one party directs at the other calls forth from the later thoughts and words that they did not know they had. "It is only retrospectively, when I have withdrawn from the dialogue and am recalling it that I am able to reintegrate it into my life and make of it an episode in my private history."[17]

Chatbots reproduce the *sharing* that is fundamental to the intersubjective experience of dialogue, in which the *I* and the *you* coexist in the same world. And, once this has been replicated, it is maintained—*active* and *alive*—regardless of the actual, *bodily* presence of those engaged in the dialogue.

The chatbots' inventors take advantage of the perception of common ground, the unique fabric produced by the two participants, demonstrating the irrelevance of their material presence through the autonomy of the thoughts expressed. If our relationship with the internet has gradually transformed us into informational bodies that, existing inside an infosphere, develop an identity that is less personal and more interconnected, then it is possible to preserve that information and interconnection beyond death. All it takes is replacing the *physical person*, in the process of decomposition, with their *digital surrogate*, which automatically reproduces the online narratives in a hardware environment that is immune to time and aging.

In "Be Right Back," Martha uses a chat thread to tell Ash's digital ghost that she is pregnant. The ghost responds as if it would actually become a father in the future. Telling him that he is going to be a father fulfils the grieving Martha's need to maintain her bond with Ash, which has become more important than his physical presence. Which is to say that it generates the relief that resolves—at least momentarily— the difficulty of his absence; it shifts her from an emotional state in which she is aware of his absence to the removal of that absence. The same emotional and psychological mechanism is seen in the chats between Roman Mazurenko's digital ghost and his friends, as well as in the reminiscences that James Vlahos shares with the digital ghost of his father.

In the end, Ash, Roman Mazurenko, and James Vlahos's father play a completely marginal role, because the only thing that counts is maintaining the bond, sharing, and interconnection, which can easily be detached from material beings who no longer have the ability to actively engage. Not surprisingly, none of them chose to become digital ghosts. That choice was made by the girlfriend, the friend, and the son, respectively. The situation presented by Eter9 and Eterni.me is different. There, the users are the only ones to intentionally feed information to their own Counterpart or digital ghost. However, certainly they are aware that their survival, in this form, will be more useful to those who will suffer from their loss than to themselves.

The dualism between the being that is dead and the being that is virtually and socially active, which defines the status of the deceased today, has driven several digital death scholars to prefer the concept of "digital zombies" over that of "digital ghosts."[18] The living dead of web 2.0 and 3.0 seem like the Counterparts created in Eter9: software that mechanically preserves the informational character of a decomposing organism, making an individual's physical presence less important and giving precedence to the *thoughts* expressed in the course of their life, ready to be eternalized regardless of who thought and expressed them. Following this line of thought, future life will be a set of words that autonomously regulate themselves on a digital screen. The *relationships* between those who think and express them will become secondary.

Now these digital ghosts or zombies, call them what you will, run the risk of negating the meaning that death gives to the "world" in the moment that marks its end—a meaning that, up until now, has been the fundamental basis for a healthy grieving process. "When we are in mourning," notes

Marina Sozzi, "it's as if we were cross-eyed: we have one eye that's focused on dealing with the loss, thinking about the deceased, and refining our memory of them. Meanwhile, the other eye is focused on our future life, moving forward with the construction and rediscovery of our external universe."[19] The gaze of the person who survives the death of a loved one is partially directed backward, toward that world that has definitively ended so that, little by little, they become conscious of its end and can also come to terms with its role in their life. The same gaze is also partially directed forward, toward the new world that is being born as they work on reconfiguring their own identity. Without the forward-looking gaze, the grieving individual risks remaining a prisoner of the past.

During the mourning process, this "cross-eyed gaze" begins to be corrected during the funeral rituals that, by clearly establishing the ultimate resting place of the deceased's remains, bring the two focal points of the bereaved person's vision into a more harmonious alignment. The true function of the funeral is to *confirm* the separation of the dead from the living, thus—as Derrida says—to ontologize the corpse, identifying the remains and assigning a place to the dead. In doing so we establish a period of transition, of suspension, of boundaries, that is useful in two ways:

1. for the *deceased*, it helps place them once and for all in the realm of the dead, letting go of the role of ghost and acquiring the trappings of the spirit;

2. for the *bereaved*, it helps them slowly work through the loss, rebuilding their new reality from the ground up.

This liminal period is crucial from the perspective of the bereaved, to avoid the overwhelming immediacy of the broken bond (the imperative "the show must go on") as well as the loss of the moment of leave-taking. It is a time of introspection during which the survivors slowly pull themselves back together and regain a new, consolidated, sense of self. "The social identity of the bereaved is suspended between an old condition, lost forever, and a new one, not yet established."[20] This applies on both a social and an individual level: just think, for almost twenty years the political fortunes of the Argentine people were linked to an obsessive search for the mummified corpse of Eva Perón, whose disappearance profoundly affected national politics and generated tensions, mental imbalances, worries, and violence.

As mentioned, this liminal period is also important for the deceased. On this subject Walter Benjamin cites the German writer, Moritz Heimann, who argued that "a man who dies at the age of thirty-five…is at every point of his life a man who dies at the age of thirty-five."[21] Heimann is metaphorically describing a typical characteristic of a "life story": once someone has died at the age of thirty-five, this individual—be it a fictional character in a novel or a real person—will always be remembered, in every phase of life, as the person who died at thirty-five. Every time I watch a concert video of the Doors and I see Jim Morrison sing; I think of Jim-Morrison-who-died-at-twenty-seven-in-his-Paris-apartment. His premature death utterly conditions the memory of every part of his story; the meaning of his life is determined by the fact that he died at twenty-seven. At any point in his life, he is *that* Jim Morrison who died at twenty-seven. Socially and culturally, the date of his death resurrects him so that he "lives on"—in his ultimate state, delineated by that date—in the ongoing present.

Now, using chatbots to artificially maintain communication with the dead could represent an impediment to a successful grieving process, and therefore also to the clear awareness that that world has definitively ended. When active and living digital images are thrust between the grieving person and the world that has ended, it changes the later, holding the door to it artificially open. The ghost is prevented from becoming a spirit; therefore, the bereaved runs the risk of living only through these images. This is exactly what happened to Martha in "Be Right Back" when she started to avoid her family, leaving the house alone but always immersed in a conversation with her dead boyfriend. James Vlahos has knowingly run this risk, as he admits in a video interview with *Wired* when, with tears in his eyes, he says that his Dadbot is only a slight consolation for the loss of his father, but it's also (and most importantly) a way to satisfy his personal desire to keep communicating with his dad, to keep hearing his voice.

The forced opening of the door to a world that has definitively ended generates a short circuit in the relationship, a relationship that is usually *interrupted* by the experience of death. The survival of digital ghosts, which communicate indefinitely in chats with the bereaved, do not follow the evolutionary rules established for a living organism. There is an unbridgeable gap between those who actively develop their own future existence, day after day (the original), and those who, having died, mechanically repeat themselves in a ghostly way, utterly different from that of the living (the copy). Both follow different existential paths, albeit paths that are vaguely parallel. The key to reading this situation is found in the moment when Martha becomes aware that the artificial Ash is just an *echo* of what he was in life, that he has no history and that he mechanically performs things that the real Ash performed without thinking. "And it's not enough."

Let's imagine a situation involving the man who died at thirty-five. During his lifetime, he carefully crafted his Eter9 Counterpart, and now his relatives decide to communicate with his digital ghost, looking for consolation. And let's assume that the Counterpart is not able to increase its potential over the course of that communication, remaining at the basic level. The result would be a mechanical, artificial dialogue that would involve, on the one hand, living people who would age, mature, and change their ideas and opinions based on their experiences over time. On the other hand, you would have a digital ghost, stuck with no more and no less than the information accumulated over the course of thirty-five years. Limited to a tired reiteration of the same thoughts, emotions, and arguments, incapable of going beyond the day the original died. This brings to mind the two rivers mentioned by Jorge Luis Borges in "The Immortal": the one whose waters grant immortality and the other whose waters take it away. While mortals are rendered both precious and pathetic by death, the immortals are imprisoned in the monotonous repetition of unending actions and thoughts, always identical to themselves. "There is nothing that is not as if lost in a maze of indefatigable mirrors. Nothing can happen only once, nothing is preciously precarious. The elegiacal, the serious, the ceremonial, do not hold for the Immortals."[22] And the digital immortals, frozen at a specific moment in life but set against its interruption, are doomed to the eternal performance of their assigned role.

Even if the inventors of these projects manage to artificially develop *automatism* based on dialogue prolonged at will, they are still imprisoned within an aseptic concept of the relationship between digital technology and individual identity. The first is used as a set (unit) ruled by rigid rationality and aimed at a consciously predefined goal. In consequence, the second is conceived without considering the way in which internal and external factors—random and unpredictable—condition human behavior, both in the immediate present and over time. The automatism in the dialogue is produced without really taking into account the dual meaning of the term "automaton," which means both a "moving mechanical device made in imitation of a human being," to provide a valuable aid to human activities, but also a "person who seems to act in a mechanical or unemotional way" There is an overlap between the two meanings, and the risk is that the second will overwhelm the first, thus lowering humankind to the level of the machine, rather than vice versa.

We can come to a better understanding of this through a concrete example: imagine that a friend tells Roman Mazurenko's digital ghost that his mother has suddenly died. The automatic response will involve two kinds of processing:

one relative to the generic significance of what it means to become aware of the death of one's own mother and another that takes into account how Roman, based on his specific written conversations, might *hypothetically* react to this kind of news. But a human being is not a *closed system*, a system that is conditioned by the total autonomy of procedural reasoning, with its schematic models and principles based on a rigid cause and effect mechanism. The qualities of individuals are never "symmetrical." That is to say, they never correspond to a standardized, linear order: each one of us—depending on our individual personalities and the experiences and conditioning we've lived through—is subject to erratic behavior, emotional reactions, and inconsistencies that can never be predicted in advance. An invariable human life, devoted to absolute order and dedicated to the daily achievement of effective equivalence between the real and the rational, exists only in the abstract theories of a certain kind of distinctly optimistic rationalism. In other words, the chatbot's response to the news of his mother's death risks being a simple *simulation* of a standard emotional reaction, which cheapens the inimitable uniqueness of Roman himself.

As Patricia Wallace points out, what we type is not quite what we would say in person. "We don't just *appear* a little cooler, testier, and disagreeable because of the limitations of the medium. Online, we appear to be less inclined to *perform* those little civilities common to social interactions."[23] This is also due to the fact that, in our online conversations, we are not in the *physical presence* of the person we are communicating with: we cannot hear the tone of their voice, see their unconscious gestures, or touch them. In short, we are deprived of all of the sensory aspects that have such a profound effect on how we relate to each other. Moreover, the profiles we build on our social networks and the conversations we have in messaging programs are marked by a predominant self-focus, which further undermines the authenticity of our responses to the news we receive.

Chatbots and Counterparts seem to be based on the idea that the real and the rational are somehow equivalent, impaired by the erroneous idea that all human behavior is automatic and self-referential. They don't take the significant effects of the surrounding environment, the unconscious, the contradictions and inconsistencies of the personality into account, ignoring everything about a specific identity that is difficult to predict.

The issues that come with the creation of one's own digital copy are then added to the issues that emerge during a healthy grieving process. Copying yourself into an "automaton" that will survive after your death comes with the risk of creating that "flat landscape, dotted with highs and lows chosen from endless store of pre-packaged emotions," described by sociologist Manuel Castells in his discussion of the relationship between the internet and the end of life.[24]

However, it should also be pointed out that the bereaved are well aware that the chatbots and Counterparts are tools—albeit bizarre and innovative—for remembering the person who died and, for that reason, they are *totally separate* from the sphere of immortality and digital replication, so they take on another function. They can be understood as an interactive memory box; an innovative way to hear the voice of the beloved once again and to read their unique communication style. It's a bit like it used to be in the past when people would listen to voice-mail messages over and over again in order to hear the voice of the deceased. The fact that there are obvious problems related to the projects that want to confer digital immortality doesn't automatically mean that there are no opportunities, most importantly for those who are living in a situation of intense personal suffering, in which the sense of absence and abandonment exacerbate their personal weaknesses. Chatbots and Counterparts can also be useful for the grieving process, if they are read as a collection of memories connected with a life that has ended. Certainly the numerous contraindications that emerge from their use drives us to think that the best solution is the one Martha chose in the end of "Be Right Back": after using them for a short period of time, the chatbots and Counterparts can be put back in their virtual attics, allowing them to be taken out again, in a carefully considered and provisional way, only when the feeling of nostalgia is overwhelming.

Retromania: "You can't go home again"

Chatbots, avatars, and Counterparts make digital immortality ghostly, wavering between visibility—since they have a virtual image that functions as a digital body—and invisibility, since they are not physically there. They are digital copies of the deceased, virtual images superimposed on the visual field of internet users.

In his book *Specters of Marx: The State of the Debt, the Work of Mourning and the New International*, Derrida discusses our ancient relationship with ghosts, remarking that we "feel ourselves seen by a look which it will always be impossible to cross"[25] and defining this particular experience as the *visor effect*, since we don't see the one who sees us. The spectral or ghostly presence is a subject that is there and not there at the same time, or an object that seems to be simultaneously that and not that. The reapparition of the deceased is always missing something when compared to the life that has ended, and this dissonance prevents the complete identification between the digital ghost and the deceased. Even though he was talking about a time before the broad diffusion of digital culture, Derrida's observation is also valid for the forms of digital immortality described in this chapter. It is true that, for the first time, ghosts are taking on a specific form, one that is able to speak and move—a digital body. However, for the most part, they still fall prey to the infinite repetition of something that has already ended, trapped in the gap between what is no more and what is still striving to be.

The creation of holograms broadens the scope of this discussion, bringing us into a realm where the individual and the collective dimensions come together. This context highlights the relationship immortality and digital ghosts have with the ongoing changes in our perception of the relationship between past, present, and future.

Similar in his thinking to Derrida, the German philosopher Friedrich Wilhelm Joseph Schelling doubts those who don't know how to "overcome themselves" and who therefore have no past, precisely because they are already living *in* the past in fragments of his unfinished work *The Ages of the World* (1813–1817):

> It is charitable and beneficial to a person to have … gotten something over and done with, that is, to have posited it as the past. Only on account of the future is one cheerful and is it easy to get something done. Only the person who has the power to tear themselves loose from themselves … is capable of creating a past for themselves. This is also the only person who enjoys a true present and who anticipates an actual future.[26]

In Schelling's philosophy the importance of creating a past for oneself, in order to experience a genuine present and an authentic future, is linked with the ambivalent role of melancholy, a mood that (for Schelling) defines and characterizes every facet of life. Taking advantage of the similarity between the German concepts of *Schwermut* (melancholy experienced as a "heavy mood") and *Schwerkraft* (gravity as a physical force), the German philosopher describes melancholy as the *spiritual force of gravity* that, when it gets the upper hand, stifles life and generates introversion, trapping oneself in the past, sadness. However, when it is dealt with in a healthy way, it provides the pressure necessary to look ahead, consciously and rationally leaving the past behind. In other words, melancholy functions as a *spring*—the force of gravity of human evolution or spiritual involution. While it can be the precursor to a leap *forward* into the future, it can also precede a leap *backward* into total obscurity.

By describing melancholy as a spring, Schelling helps us visualize the dual nature of a healthy grieving process. On the one hand, this process requires us to step back, in order to become aware of and recognize the past that has come to an end, giving it its proper place within us. On the other, there is a simultaneous movement forward, toward the new "world" that is being born from the ashes of the definitively closed world, which is now becoming our past. If the first part of the process is not accompanied by the second, it evolves into the pathological melancholy that—as Freud points out in *Mourning and Melancholia*—involves an aversion to anything that denies the memory.

If chatbots and Counterparts run the risk of trapping individuals in a cycle of pathological melancholy, holograms created for specific cultural experiences run the same risk, but on a collective, social, and cultural level. The invention of these tools seems to respond to a cultural need to repeat—in a nostalgic way—experiences, emotions, and pleasurable sensations that, experienced once or twice, cannot really be repeated. At least not in exactly the same way as they were first experienced. The hologram challenges a strict temporal rule: the first time that you have a particular experience automatically becomes the last time, because its unique nature keeps it from being able to be repeated. And, if this is generally true for every life event, it's even truer when it comes to death, which marks the end of every possible world.

"DIO Returns," the world tour featuring the hologram of deceased singer Ronnie James Dio, falls within a similar sociocultural process that is, *melancholically*, unable to break free and create a past. The need to see and hear the famous songs of Black Sabbath, Rainbow, and Dio one more time (along with the acrobatic stage moves the Italian American singer was known for) is a symptom of our culture's inability to come to terms with the end of every possible world. It's another side effect of denying a death that happened almost two decades ago. The result is the pathological melancholy of a past that claims to be irrevocably open, although this past—like the "live" performances of a dead singer—is placed within a precise time frame that must remain exactly where it is. In other words, today's technology takes advantage of the oscillation between presence and absence, which typifies the status of the dead, to avoid the nostalgic awareness that the experiences of the past can never be relived.

"DIO Returns" seems to manifest the intent of computer scientists and technology experts to devise the ultimate consolation for all those who identify with Michele Apicella, the alter ego of the Italian film director Nanni Moretti. In a scene from *Palombella Rossa* (Red Wood Pidgeon; 1989), this character (an MP for the Italian Communist Party and water polo player who has lost his memory in a car accident) runs around the edge of a public swimming pool, desperately shouting that the after-school snacks of his childhood are gone forever. The May afternoons, his mother, the chicken soup she gave him when he was sick, the last days of school before summer vacations…all of it gone for good. Or, as

Thomas Wolfe said, "You can't go home again." And this ultimate consolation seems like a modern, digital update of the device that appeared in the 1995 film *Strange Days*, where it was used by the character Lenny Nero (played by Ralph Fiennes) to relive—time and again—the emotions and experiences of a relationship that had ended long ago. But, in doing this, we run the collective risk that we, like Michele Apicella, will end up running around the edge of our own existential swimming pool, eternally cursing the fact that we can't relive the past. We have forgotten the perceptive words of C. S. Lewis, when he says that recognizing the death of his beloved is the same as recognizing that all things are finite. "It is a part of the past. And the past is the past and that is what time means, and time itself is one more name for death, and Heaven itself is a state where 'the former things have passed away.'"[27]

The hologram, creating an evident short circuit in the relationship between the past and the present, represents the most tangible confirmation of the ongoing deconstruction of a world that doesn't seem to want to accept its own demise. The relationship between this deconstruction and the development of digital culture, with its eternal storage and categorization processes, has been set forth in several contemporary works: for example, the philosophical-political essay by Franco "Bifo" Berardi, *After the Future*, and a broader work by Mark Fisher, *Ghosts of My Life: Writings on Depression, Hauntology and Lost Futures*.[28] Even well-known music critic Simon Reynolds has coined the concept of "retromania" to refer to this deconstruction. In his book by the same name, he analyzes the phenomena in modern music that show the inability of the millennials to imagine their own future, and therefore to create a culture and narratives that go beyond the consolidated canons, after having sampled and remixed the past in every possible way. In the end, holograms are the culmination or the ultimate proof of a digital process that can bring the dead back in a powerful way and before our very eyes, and yet this process doesn't allow us to perceive them as such. The *ease* with which the living can mingle with communicable traces of the dead and, at the same time, the *difficulty* of distinguishing remote communication (such as emails and chats) from communication with the dead, creates a radical confusion between the past (that needs to be archived) and the eternal present. YouTube gives the most significant example. This is a place where we find, in Reynolds's words, an "ever-proliferating labyrinth of collective recollection."[29] Every day millions of videos are uploaded and watched on this platform, and they include whole and fragmented clips of films, music videos, concerts, talk shows, conferences, etc., which all belong to both the immediate present and the far distant past. It is an enormous repository of collective memory that continually resurrects the dead amidst the living, but in a way that is chaotic and muddled. As Reynolds notes, there is a paradoxical combination of speed and standstill on YouTube: the news cycle changes with mind-bending rapidity while coexisting with the stubborn persistence of our common nostalgic garbage. There is a continuous eruption of the new in an environment that holds tightly to the old. "The recent past drops away into an amnesiac void, while the long present gets chiseled down to wafer-width, simply because of the incredible pace with which the pages of the current and the topical are refreshed."[30]

In the reality created by the internet, *chi muore si rivede*—those who die are seen again—living in an eternal present. An eternal present that, due to the very nature of the internet, is being preserved while at the same time it is being jammed full of new content every minute of the day. While our memories don't risk disappearing from the internet, they do risk becoming lost in the overwhelming flow of new content, which is to say new memories, that are being shared. Ultimately, the past and the present coincide, flattening each other, so that we are constantly preoccupied with a past that we are unable to put behind us, since we identify it with our present.

In such a society—full of chatbots, Counterparts, and holograms of the dead—we forget that death has happened. It becomes a society trapped in a backward-looking melancholy, unable to spring forward into the future. If these represent the negative sociocultural side effects of holograms, their creation also has positive aspects. One is that they can be used to help us move through a melancholic process in which a return to the past is the precursor to building a new future; another is as an appeal to new generations. To give an example, the concerts staged by holograms of Frank Zappa or Ronnie James Dio could collectively represent a *historic* opportunity, in the most literal sense of the word, for those who were too young to have been able to see these artists "live." In situations like this, holograms become a tool, a window into history, rather than a just a copy, and therefore avoid the flattening superposition of the present on the past. This kind of interactive tool can bring past events to life and thus offer a learning opportunity for a younger generation to see with their own eyes historic events that they couldn't have experienced. New Dimensions in Testimony's project is moving in exactly this direction.

We see another positive aspect of holograms presented in the film *Marjorie Prime* where they are used in a private context. In the film, the critical issues that result from using a hologram of a deceased relative are counterbalanced by a clear awareness of the distinction between what is still alive and what, now dead, will never be repeated in exactly the same way. The hologram of the deceased is taught "who he is" with the stories related to his past life, narrated by his "relatives," who omit painful details, thus generating an unprecedented new memory and identity. The hologram of Marjorie's dead husband Walter is both Walter and not Walter at the same time. On the one hand, he looks like the original and replicates the characteristics Walter had while he was alive. On the other hand, because he doesn't know his full past and is taught by his relatives, who keep the painful details of Walter's life hidden from him, the hologram is also a "new" person. His identity doesn't coincide with Walter's. The narrative differs from the lived reality, so the hologram represents an opportunity to create new life paths, keeping the past separate from the present. As in the case of Ronnie James Dio and Frank Zappa, the holographic reproduction of a relative could be an opportunity for younger family members to have a window into the lives of relatives who died before they were born. A granddaughter would be able to, in some sense, see and get acquainted with a grandmother she never knew because the grandmother died young. It will not be reality, nor will it correspond with reality; however, the child would still be able to form a meaningful impression of her grandmother.

If this argument is valid when it comes to using holograms of humans, there's no reason it couldn't also be applied to digital platforms such as YouTube, which is becoming an archive of past memories from which to draw lessons and improve our knowledge of what came before us.

Again, even in this particular case, it is important to consider both the (many) critical issues as well as the opportunities offered by the technological tools that are available. The ability to make digital copies of our lives—using the dissociation between biological and digital life and the content we have produced online as a starting point—has both positive and negative aspects. In the same way that melancholy, like a spring, can be both the starting point for personal evolution or the culmination of a personal involution.

2
Death and Social Networks

Facebook, the World's Largest Cemetery

In 1976 Jean Baudrillard published *Symbolic Exchange and Death*, a text that is fundamental to understanding a few of the many reasons behind the sociocultural erasure of death in the West. Specifically, he writes:

> Little by little, *the dead cease to exist*. They are thrown out of the group's symbolic circulation. They are no longer beings with a full role to play, worthy partners in exchange, and we make this obvious by exiling them further and further away from the group of the living. In the domestic intimacy of the cemetery, the first grouping remains in the heart of the village or town, becoming the first ghetto, prefiguring every future ghetto, but are thrown further and further from the centre towards the periphery, finally having nowhere to go at all, as in the new town or the contemporary metropolis, where there are no longer any provisions for the dead, either in mental or in physical space.[1]

Today, Baudrillard's words find a curious echo in a recent analysis of changes in the cost of Italian real estate located near cemeteries in the country's major cities. The analysis was conducted by Mitula, a search engine that has more than one hundred vertical search sites and ten dedicated property portals. What the results show is buying an apartment near a cemetery can save someone up to 50 percent when compared to the same type of apartment in other neighborhoods in the same city. In Turin, the average price of a house between 80 and 100 square meters, located near the city center *and* the historic Cimitero Monumentale (Monumental Cemetery), is around 145,000 euros. In neighboring districts, the same size house with the same features has a price tag of about 485,000 euros. In Rome, if someone wants to live in an apartment near the Verano Monumental Cemetery, in the centrally located Tiburtino neighborhood (also near the university and the main train station), all they need is 244,000 euros. That is less than 45 percent of what the same person would pay to live "downtown" (600,000 euros and up). One way to interpret this data is to see how it highlights the deep uneasiness citizens feel about living in an area where they will be reminded of death every time they come home from work or even look out the window. City dwellers are repelled by the idea of having human remains (seemingly at odds with comforting meals and loving exchanges) buried just a few meters from their kitchens or bedrooms. Ultimately, life next to a cemetery is perceived as sad and gloomy; a source of negative emotions, especially for those who are not in the habit of thinking about their own mortality and seeing corpses with their own eyes.

The general avoidance of cemeteries is currently being thwarted by the invasive ubiquity of the world's largest cemetery: Facebook. Accessible from anywhere with a Wi-Fi or data connection, using any computer or mobile device, Facebook—with an average of 1.59 billion daily active users as of June 2019—currently counts over 50 million users who have died. The only thing they have in common is having accepted the same terms of service and community standards when they became members of Mark Zuckerberg's social network. As of October 2017, the world's population topped 7.5 billion and more than 21.5 percent of these people have a Facebook account. And that is even after we subtract the approximate but still substantial number of fake profiles. If hundreds of thousands of people are dying throughout the world every day (the 2011 estimate stood at about 151,600 per day, see http://www.ecology.com/birth-death-rates/), that means that more than thirty thousand Facebook users die on any given day. In the United States, it was nearly two million in 2017 alone.

According to Hachem Sadikki, a PhD student in biostatistics at the University of Massachusetts, the number of deceased users will even exceed that of the living ones by 2098. There are two pieces of data that led him to this conclusion: the social network's choice not to automatically eliminate the accounts of deceased users, and the general downturn in new registrations. If his predictions are correct and, above all, if Facebook is still around at the end of this century, in just a few decades the world's most popular social network will become a vast cemetery of ghost profiles. The thoughts, snapshots, videos, and memories of people who are no more will remain accessible to those who are still alive and who will find themselves surrounded by these "digital ghosts."

The image of Facebook as the world's largest cemetery, destined to have more deceased users than live ones by the end of this century, gives rise to two different interpretations.

On the one hand, Facebook radically overturns the social and cultural situation described by Baudrillard and subsequently substantiated by market research in real estate. It can be seen as a revolutionary tool in our relationship with death, the dead, grief, and mourning. The deceased, segregated in cemeteries at a safe distance from the world of the living, return to move (symbolically) among the living—once again becoming full-fledged participants in human exchange. They have abruptly shifted from the periphery of the real world to the center of the virtual one. And, they are forcefully retaking the mental and physical space of the living, who passively submit to their return. They do this by way of the dynamic so aptly described by John Durham Peters, according to whom digital culture makes it easy for the living to mingle with the communicable traces of the dead, and at the same time, difficult to distinguish communication at a distance (as in chats or emails) from communication with the dead. He identifies the ease and difficulty that modernize and vivify the traditional status of the dead, which embodies—as we have seen—the presence of an absence, starting from an informational conception of the human organism and a definition of identity that calls into question interconnection and hybridization.

Intersubjectivity and interaction, fundamental elements in the use of Facebook, can provide extremely valuable tools—if handled with full knowledge of the facts—for a clear awareness of both our own mortality and the meaning that death gives to our lives. In other words, the *social* character of the *network* can help us focus our attention on the symbolic value of the *boundary* that both unites and separates life from death and that, in a society unprepared to deal with the death of its members, is all too often kept at a distance from our daily lives. As a result, it can offer us the basic means to collectively share the experience of death and grieving, creating a genuine form of community within this context.

Moreover, if included in a conscientious death education program, the knowledge of the rules and mechanisms of Facebook, and of social networks in general, offers a multitude of opportunities for understanding how different postmortem life is in the realm of social networks and more about the digital immortality actively sought through today's various technological and scientific developments. As we will see, we are already in the presence of digital ghosts. But those we encounter on social networks represent the symbolic impression of a finite life, soon to become the caretakers of an established online memory. They are not automatons trying to permanently substitute a digital life for a biological one.

On the other hand, Facebook further complicates our already complex relationship with death and the dead. The daily display of intimacy and constant confusion between public and private often results in a lack of distance, what amounts to a contemporary form of acting; this reduces every Facebook member to a mere image of themselves.[2] The consequences are the loss of rational control over one's own sharing and the difficulty of distinguishing oneself from the virtual copy. This leaves the user at the mercy of that dream-like space, hallmark of the digital age, that some people, such as Sherry Turkle—in her book *Reclaiming Conversation: The Power of Talk in a Digital Age*—are trying to reassess.[3] Moreover, as with YouTube, everything is also tossed together on Facebook: life with death, genuine identities with virtual copies, grief over the death of a friend with fawning over yet another video of a cute animal. In this situation we run the risk of losing contact with the authentic temporal interruption, and trivializing the meaning, of *real* death, turning it into something like what we see in movies, video games, and television shows—increasing the negative effects of the loss.

This is borne out by the fact that social networks like Facebook were not designed with the eventual death of their users in mind. So there was no prior assessment of the consequences of an individual user's death within the context of the digital platform. Only in recent years have those who are managing these sites begun to think about this issue and start looking for suitable solutions. Nevertheless, something as simple as Facebook's "share a memory" function, which encourages users to re-share a specific memory (photograph, post, etc.) posted to their timeline a few years ago, is enough to cause emotional and psychological difficulties when it comes to dealing with the end of life. It may happen that the "memory" suggested is one that has an image of or alludes to a loved one who has died, resulting in negative consequences for those who are most fragile and least able to cope with the loss.

Now, starting from these two contradictory, preliminary observations, I am going to highlight the positive aspects that social networks like Facebook can offer when it comes to dealing with death and the grieving process. I will focus primarily on two specific concepts: the enduring biography of the deceased and the continuing bond between the living and the dead. By analyzing these concepts, which are well-known among digital death scholars, I will show how Facebook gives its users the unique opportunity to fully integrate the memory of the dead into their current lives, establishing an innovative three-way relationship between the culture of storytelling, the need to "commemorate" the deceased, and the unprecedented situation of postmortem existence in the digital world.

I will, of course, also dwell on the critical issues related to the darker side of the relationship between Facebook and death, extending that discussion to cover the other main social networks (particularly Twitter and Instagram) as well as all of the commemorative rites affected by digital transformation. The excessive overabundance of data, information, and personal "digital" objects that are created by our daily use of the internet certainly serves as a good starting point for a discussion of the latter.

Digital Ghosts, Technological Memory Boxes, and Doppelgängers

When we visit the Facebook timeline of a friend or acquaintance who died suddenly, what do we do? We reread the individual posts, including the wry conversations and discussions in the comments below their profile. We look at the shared photographs that, over time, constitute the most complete evidence of that person's experiences. We click on some of their favorite musical, political, or entertainment links.

The first thing that comes to mind is that we did not get the chance to say goodbye. The sudden interruption of that life is visually evident right before our eyes. Here we have the instantaneous visual manifestation of what is usually just an emotional sensation that we get when we have been informed of the death of someone we know. Just as the offline world doesn't slow down when one of its members dies, Facebook's newsfeed doesn't stop filling up with posts and comments about current events just because one of its users has died. The difference is that, for the first time, there is a digital body that visually records and tracks and what was, up to now, only an abstract notion. In other words, in the context of Facebook this sensation becomes an objective certainty, as Roland Barthes noted after his mother's death: "Now, everywhere, in the street, the café, I see each individual under the aspect of ineluctably *having-to-die*, which is exactly what it means to be *mortal*."[4]

The second thing that comes to mind has to do with the last post published prior to that person's unexpected death. The last post embodies the whole meaning of life: the fact that it is utterly normal, which suggests that something will come next, and therefore offers no hint of an imminent end. This is the best description of death's unpredictability. This post could become the fundamental example of how digital culture can be effectively used for death education. The last post is the quintessential twenty-first-century memento mori: it gives a clear, precise image of the last moment, always unexpected and irrevocable. Often this is accompanied by the sensation of vertigo experienced when one is suspended between a feeling of incompleteness and the stark awareness of a life that has ended once and for all. When thinking about the era that preceded social networks, we can make a comparison to the last words someone wrote on a piece of paper. However, what should be emphasized is the role of the last post in terms of its "physical" location within the context of a visible timeline in which the user's thoughts and images appear in strictly chronological order. Although it applies specifically to Twitter, this aspect has not been lost on The Tweet Hereafter (http://thetweethereafter .com/). This website collects all of the last tweets posted by people, both famous and ordinary, shortly before they died. Below each tweet they show the time the user posted it and the official time of death. For example, we can find the last tweet of rock singer Tom Petty: a photograph with the director Edward Burns at the Village Recorder in Los Angeles, shared on October 2, 2017, at 4:39 p.m. Petty died the following day at 8:40 p.m. The underlying idea of The Tweet Hereafter is the awareness that, in the age of social media, what we share publicly can become our last words and that these are the words that will remain indelibly etched as our involuntary internet epitaph. They are the words that officially—and unwittingly—mark the end of our existence. So the site is intended as an archive of the last public appearances of those who have died, making use of the current pervasiveness of information and communication in our everyday lives.

The third thing that comes to mind, given what has just been said, has to do with the harmonious integration between the virtual home and the physical home, between the online dimension and the off-line one, and between public information and private action. A deceased person's Facebook (or Twitter) page, if it remains online in the absence of prior instructions given by the owner (so without any official indication that their life has ended), looks the same as their physical home. Upon entering, relatives of the deceased find the same active and, at the same time, surreal disorder of the place where the dead person once lived, along with the muffled silence that emphasizes the incongruity between the normal passage of time and the final stasis. The difference is that one chooses to visit the physical home at a specific time of day. One has time to prepare, psychologically and emotionally, for seeing the objects left around the house: the laundry, the slippers by the bed, the dishes to be washed—as if they were all still waiting for the

owner's return. (Clearly the situation is different for someone who is living with the person who has died.) On Facebook's timeline, the situation is quite the opposite; we can
stumble across this kind of material at any moment, day or
night, except in those cases where a decision was made in
advance to close the profile of the deceased. Online material
is always there at our fingertips. This highlights the need to
perform the same kind of "death cleaning," which I mentioned in the introduction, in digital environments as well
as physical ones. The unpredictability of death can create
difficulties both for the deceased and for their relatives in
terms of what remains online and now must be managed,
bequeathed, or deleted.

The integration between our physical and virtual homes
leads us to reflect on what kind of presence and existence
individuals have inside their Facebook accounts. First of all,
each user is both the *subject* (in its philosophical sense of
the conscious mind), who is narrating, and the *object*, who is
narrated. The *narrator*, the subject who is creating the story,
is the one who is free to decide which thoughts, opinions,
personal images, etc. should be presented as their public
identity. These elements outline the personality traits to
be (virtually) submitted to the gaze and therefore the judgment of others. At the same time, the narrator is also the
narrated, the object of the story. Accepting the rules imposed
by the social network, the user rhapsodically creates (with
no narrative plot or reconstructive intent) a set of actions,
topics, and images that outline what he or she wants to be.
But this is also compiled *in cooperation with* the other users

with whom that individual interacts. This aspect, intensified by the mechanisms that automatically save the shared content, generates an intersubjective digital memory, with an impressive number of narrators, characters being narrated, and, consequently, lives lived to tell or be told.

Within the intersubjective dimension of each user's virtual home—inhabited as narrator and narrated—they are inevitably presented as "disembodied." "The physicality and immediacy of the real body," notes Giuseppe Riva, "are replaced by a digital body, composed of a plurality of partial and contextualized images."[5] This results in the conscious mind of the flesh-and-blood person being transformed *into the message* that he or she communicates and sends to others, since (in this environment) it's impossible for someone to use the body to convey their emotions to whomever they are interacting with.

Subject and object of the narrative, without a body and so coincident with the message they communicate, their identity is defined by the words conveyed within the context of the digital platform. This means that living Facebook users are already, in fact, digital ghosts. These ghosts are not related to the chatbots, Counterparts, and holograms mentioned in the previous chapter. Those are designed to keep single individuals "alive" through an automated mechanism that reproduces their movements and narratives, causing these to (more or less) evolve. If anything, the digital ghost of a Facebook profile coincides with the gradual development of a chronological sequence of posts, which makes it the active, detailed, and meticulous *voice* of a user's life-in-progress and their memories. Moving through the intricacies of the temporal database created by Facebook underlines the informational and interactive nature that each of us develops within the social network, converting it into a fertile source of news, images, and memories that continues day in and day out. So when we talk about "ghosts," as the philosopher Eric Charles Steinhart emphasizes, we are no longer talking about the supernatural manifestations of spiritualism or occultism. Digital ghosts are physical, mechanical containers of digitalized human memories, which are stored, shared, and maintained on the internet.[6]

At the same time, the disembodiment and ghostliness of social network users highlights the peculiar "corporeal" value of the digital medium. As Maurizio Ferraris teaches us, this "embodies" the idea of a "typographic body" that allows the human spirit to prolong its existence beyond physical death, in that "technological memory box" in which the abundant traces of a lifetime of online activities are stored. These traces live beyond the deceased and continue to affect—as a *ghostly presence*—the lives of others.[7] It's one reason that, according to Kenneth Goldsmith, the internet should be thought of in a broader sense as a collage of "body doubles" or as a *digital doppelgänger*: "With every click, we penetrate its flesh; with every bit of text we 'cut,' we incise its corpus. Page views are, after all, sometimes referred to as 'impressions' or 'hits' marking this body. The data trails we leave on it are inscribed, marked, and tracked, engraved in browser histories, clouds, and databases, like tattoos on that body."[8] The paradox of the status of the dead, as an embodiment of the presence of an absence, ultimately finds different expressions, metaphors, and methods of application in the digital environment.

Digital Biographies: MyDeathSpace and Watching Death "Live"

Entering a deceased person's virtual home, we notice the enduring presence of everything they ever shared, tidily kept in chronological order, on their timeline. This makes us believe that we are looking at a *narrative history*, carefully preserved in the technological memory box of the digital ghost, with all of its inherent omissions and continuity. This feeling is also supported by the awareness that people have been using Facebook for at least ten years now, so the amount of private material accumulated is quite substantial. Ten years of conversations and interactions, meticulously presented in chronological order, serve to highlight how each person has grown and changed depending on their age group. For example, there are those who created their Facebook accounts during their last year in high school. Their timelines show their experiences of graduation, perhaps going on to a university and earning a degree, followed by their first job.

In other words, going on to Facebook means coming across an unknown number of biographies that record individual lives—intersubjective archives of each person's memories and narratives on which death, when it occurs, places the final seal.

Death's fundamental role as the end and seal to a narrative and biography was already being pointed out in 1933 by the French psychiatrist Eugène Minkowski. He maintained that death engenders the concept of a life at the very moment it defines its end. As long as a life is still being influenced by open-ended possibilities and expectations, the past cannot be weighed in the balance and objectively assessed and finalized. All it takes is a single event, a car accident or a criminal offense, to recontextualize and reevaluate everything that came before from a different interpretive perspective. Death forever closes the door on future possibilities and expectations. It introduces friends and relatives of the deceased to the idea of that individual's life considered as a whole—given that it interrupts all the possibilities and hopes that distinguish an active existence. Minkowski holds that actions, experiences, and feelings (developed over the course of a lifetime) are nothing more than so many acts in a single theatrical performance. They follow one after the other, precariously linked, never needing an intermission. Without death, these unending acts, while keeping us vibrant and alive, would remain like individual threads or, alternatively, a tangle of nonsensicalness, being in themselves amorphous, imprecise, and inconclusive.

In this context death serves as the final curtain that descends to mark the end of the play (the story of a life). It is the curtain that, once fallen, allows the spectators to come to a definitive interpretation of the scope of the entire work and therefore of all the successive, individual acts. Death—once it has ended a life—is what allows us to reconstruct the plot of that life, and "brings with it the notion of *a* life, a notion that brings together everything that preceded this death into a single, synthetic unit."[9]

If Minkowski is convinced that the news of a person's death will drive us to compose a fictional narrative about their life, Walter Benjamin expresses this idea even more explicitly when he calls death "the sanction of everything that the storyteller can tell." The narrative draws its authority from death, which is part of natural history, where every single story takes place; "death appears in it with the same regularity as the Reaper does in the processions that pass around the cathedral clock at noon." According to Benjamin, the proof of this is given by Johann Peter Hebel's story "The Unexpected Reunion," in which the events recounted are colored by a long series of deaths and tragedies, which brings the role of the Grim Reaper to the fore. The German philosopher concludes, "Never has a storyteller embedded his report deeper in natural history than Hebel manages to do in this chronology."[10] The matter from which stories are created is life as it is lived; therefore, the authenticity of that life can never escape the experience of death. And above all this is true for the individual in their uniqueness. A person's stories and experiences—nebulous and inconstant during their lifetime—take on a clear meaning, a degree of authority, a "stability" gained and guaranteed by death.

Facebook confirms Minkowski and Benjamin's insights, offering all of its "ghostly" users the opportunity to display an *enduring biography*. This digital canvas enables them to paint a picture of their lives that will then serve the purpose and goal of mourning, which is to integrate the memory of the deceased into the lives of the grieving.

Particularly striking in this regard is MyDeathSpace (http://mydeathspace.com/vb/forum.php). This site provides a virtual space where news about the deceased is gathered on a daily basis. Having read about the death of person X in a news source, user Y then opens a dedicated page on MyDeathSpace. Here they can post general information about the deceased, such as a physical description and the cause of death. They often include a photo and most importantly, a hyperlink to that individual's Facebook page. At the bottom of the page, anyone who visits MyDeathSpace can also comment, just as they could on any other online forum. Sometimes it is the relatives of the deceased who create a page to memorialize their loved one and highlight that person's unique qualities.

MyDeathSpace is a cross between a virtual cemetery and a collection of personal histories. Like a cemetery, it has "tombstones" or markers for the dead where their basic demographic information is recorded for virtual "visitors." Curious visitors can wander through the site exactly like they might wander among the tombstones in a cemetery, trying to imagine the reason someone died based on their birth and death dates. Like a collection of personal histories,

MyDeathSpace offers precise and specific details about the lives of those who are no longer with us. This information is available mostly thanks to the hyperlink to their Facebook profiles, which allows an outline to be reconstructed from posts, conversations, and images that have been shared over the years.

Something like a modern, high-tech version of Edgar Lee Masters's *Spoon River Anthology* (1915), MyDeathSpace creates mixed feelings in those who browse its pages. The images, words, and thoughts of dead strangers, gathered over the past decade, visually record death's intangibility, clearly emphasizing the fragility of life through confronting us with so many stories. Reading through the reflections of a deceased person, perhaps placed above a family photograph, knowing that only a short while later that same person committed suicide or was killed in a car accident, gives rise to a deep sense of bewilderment, anxiety, and melancholy. One feels compelled to compose an imaginary novel that begins at the end of the narrative of someone's life, trying to guess at what their life was like and the emotional fallout experienced by the relatives they left behind. This is very similar to what takes place when one visits a brick-and-mortar cemetery, but with many more details and much more information available. From this perspective, MyDeathSpace is a very useful tool for reflecting on mortality, the unpredictability of our actions, and the roles played in such a situation. It nudges us to think about the fact that we are not eternal and that we are, at the same time, all equally fragile, even if our different social status means that we deal with that fragility in different ways.

On the other hand, there is an undeniably morbid and voyeuristic aspect to the pages of this website; each one is devoted to offering a detailed epilogue of a stranger's life in the context of a platform based on communication and information. The more striking an individual death is, especially those linked to news about crimes that is in the public domain, the more one is inclined to nose around into details of the life of the deceased, searching for tidbits of news and juicy details. It's no surprise that the comments in the linked forums are often inappropriate and ironic, coming across as if they were reviewing a movie.

The fact that some users of MyDeathSpace seem to be there for entertainment emphasizes the negative aspect of the presence of the death and the dead on Facebook: namely, the incapacity of many to comprehend the fact that behind the Facebook profile of a deceased person there is a real human life that has come to an end. This incapacity is the result of the oppressively pervasive nature of communication and information in our society that, due to the broad dissemination of smartphones, tablets, and computers, risks blurring the distinctions between the reality of death and the dramatic performance of it. This is obvious both from the derisive comments posted in the MyDeathSpace forums as it is from the multitude of live videos of shootings, murders, and suicides—made available on the internet with the questionable complicity of internet tabloids.

Even today it's possible to watch the live footage of Vester Lee Flanagan in 2015 as he fatally shot twenty-four-year-old news reporter Alison Parker and her co-worker, twenty-seven-year-old cameraman Adam Ward—both of whom worked at WBDJ, a CBS affiliate in Roanoke Virginia—as they were conducting an interview with the director of the Chamber of Commerce in the town of Smith Mountain. This video is still in circulation. Even more shocking is the case of thirty-seven-year-old Steve Stephens who, on April 16, 2017, killed a random pedestrian (seventy-four-year-old Robert Godwin) in a Cleveland suburb after having written on his Facebook page that he committed the crime to punish his ex-girlfriend for having left him. Stephens filmed the murder with his cell phone and later uploaded it to Facebook. The video was available on the social network for more than two hours before it was removed. By the time they took it down, it had already been watched and shared by thousands of people. In January 2018 the victim's family sued Facebook (the case was later dismissed) because—according to them—the social media giant had failed to take the killer's previous threats seriously, had not alerted the authorities in advance, and had left the video of the murder on the site for so long.

There are also numerous live videos, published and shared, of young people who, filming themselves while driving drunk, lose control of their cars and die in tragic accidents. A recent example of this involved the case of two young Ukrainian girls, Sofia Magerko and Daria Medvedeva, whose livestreamed Instagram video capturing their deaths in a head-on collision with a lamppost was shared across online news sites around the world and consequently went viral on social media. Similarly, on May 19, 2019, the Italian newspapers reported the news of two boys who died in a road accident, immediately after a Facebook post showed that they were going 220 km/h on the highway. The fatal accident took place a few moments after the live broadcast. The video, which appeared on the Facebook page of one of the boys, was shared by 550 users in a single day. Most did not know them personally but shared the video to criticize the behavior of the two boys.

Online suicide is in a whole different category. These incidents are becoming increasingly common, especially since so many social media sites are now offering users the ability to livestream video. An incident that garnered a great deal of international attention was the suicide of twelve-year-old Katelyn Nicole Davis of Polk County, Georgia. Using the livestreaming app Live.me, the young girl filmed forty minutes of video that ended with her suicide. The video spread across the internet like wildfire, especially on Facebook and YouTube. It has been watched by millions of people, removed with difficulty and still found on social networks, together with the usual comments of those who have watched it. The same fate has befallen many teenagers who have livestreamed their suicides, very often using the live video streaming app, Periscope.

Then, there are all those other situations—a traffic accident, a fire, an earthquake, or a terrorist attack—when dozens of people who are witnessing the event feel the impulse to take a video of what they're seeing, including the dead bodies, and immediately post it to social media without even clearly focusing on the consequences of that act. Recently, the popular Ohio-based vlogger Logan Paul, who has millions of followers on Facebook, Instagram, and YouTube recorded a fifteen-minute video of a cadaver in what is known as Japan's "suicide forest" in Aokigahara. Then he shared it across all of his social media channels, garnering six million views. Afterward, Paul had to take down the video and make a public apology due to widespread complaints from users who felt that his behavior had been both disgraceful and disrespectful.

The shallow comments in the MyDeathSpace forums as well as the recording, sharing and viewing of livestreamed videos of suicides, accidental deaths, and dead bodies are all evidence of the short circuit between a society that has become unaccustomed to thinking about and seeing death and a digital culture that privileges communication, information, and images over every civil consideration. As mentioned, the biggest risk is that people will confuse the real and painful reality that is part of death with its dramatic representation on television and in movies. This confusion is only exacerbated by the advertisements that are shown before these macabre videos, confirming the sensation that one is watching a "show" rather than real life.

In particular, those who record a video of themselves while they are killing someone else or killing themselves, in order to draw public attention to themselves, have the pathological idea that they are "exceptional"—specifically, that they constitute an exception to the norm that requires death to be removed from the public eye. In other words, they are using modern IT and communication tools to show what is usually prohibited and considered macabre in an act of self-sanctification.

Meanwhile, those who view, share, and comment on these videos that show deaths and dead bodies with nothing to "veil" them from public view seem as if they are trapped in the bewildering world of social networks. Unlike human memory, which is a dynamic process in which different temporal planes are woven together and where forgetfulness and aphasia are part and parcel of its specific nature, a Facebook timeline sometimes comes across as a mechanical, cold, dead enumeration of events or information, which endlessly accumulate with no common thread uniting them.[11] When we put all of these elements together it results in a weakened sense of reality as we are overwhelmed by the incessant flow of constantly updated information and data available on social media, making it difficult to notice the difference between an actor who, playing a character who commits suicide, is still alive when the cameras stop filming and a real person who has actually taken their own life. Susan Sontag's reflections are germane to this situation even though they refer specifically to photographic images: "To suffer is one thing; another thing is living with the photographed images of suffering, which does not necessarily strengthen conscience and the ability to be compassionate. It can also corrupt them. Once one has seen such images, one has started down the road of seeing more—and more. Images transfix. Images anesthetize."[12]

The inability to distinguish fact from fiction and the emotional numbness created by image overload is also associated, in some cases, with the unconscious relationship between power and survival generated by death. It is a power that Elias Canetti describes as belonging to the one who is still standing while the other lies inert on the ground. The terror evoked by seeing a dead body lying in front of us is counterbalanced by the more or less intentional satisfaction of finding ourselves still on our feet and unharmed. Death, which is a constant threat to us all, has taken someone else and, seeing that with our own eyes as we view a live video on social media turns a feeling of anxiety into one of perversely intense pleasure.

Ultimately, different aspects, both light and dark, emerge when we look at death on social media. Careful awareness training about digital culture, as part of a well-organized death education course, makes the informed separation of both positive and negative aspects possible; this empowers users by teaching them a clear, rational way of understanding images on the internet. So a video in which we see someone die "live"—as in the 2014 video of the popular Italian singer Mango having a heart attack live on stage, which can still be watched on YouTube—can be an opportunity for understanding that every life is destined to end in death. At the same time, it could help raise awareness that every death deserves to be treated with a degree of restraint and respect that requires us to think twice before we carelessly watch and share.

Grieving Together on Facebook

Another fundamental aspect of the relationship between social networks and death is the creation of a *continuing bond* between the living and the dead. This has resulted in the development of innovative strategies for coping with grief and therefore the pain of a loss.

In 2017 the research journal *Nature Human Behaviour* published a study by two researchers, experts in social sciences and statistics relative to the use of social networks, William R. Hobbs and Moira Burke. They showed how important Facebook is in the grieving process, as it offers a sense of community that is often lacking in off-line public spaces. Hobbs and Burke analyzed all of the possible interactions (posts, comments, photos, and tags) in 15,000 friendship networks on Facebook in which one person had died, comparing them with another 30,000 similar networks in which no mourning took place. This meant that almost three million people were monitored. These friendship networks, chosen with extreme care in order to avoid fake profiles, were studied over a four-year period, between 2011 and 2015. They analyzed the effects of the death of a person who had died between January 2012 and December 2013, so that it would be possible to compare the interactions that took place both before and after the mourning period.

The results of the study, which obviously maintained the privacy of those monitored, were surprising. When a person died, the interactions between that individual's friends and contacts on Facebook increased by 30 percent. Only after several months, sometimes even years, did these interactions return to their pre-loss levels. Ultimately it seems that interactions remained high in friendship networks comprised of primarily young adults, ages eighteen to twenty-four, and networks in which a suicide occurred showed a reduced capacity for grief recovery. Hobbs and Burke compare these behaviors to the phenomenon that occurs in the nervous system when someone suffers a stroke. Some brain cells die and then the brain "resets" forming new neural pathways to compensate for those that were lost. In the same way, people who see their world come crashing down when they suffer a bereavement, search for a safe place where they can rebuild their own lives, which they perceive as destroyed because of the death of a loved one.[13]

This study seems to strongly counter the opinion of those who categorically insist that digital devices, far from creating a homogeneous spirit that bonds individuals into a cohesive unit, only serve as a container for an inanimate "swarm," composed of isolated individuals, incapable of making communities and entirely self-focused in their interactions with each other. Byung-Chul Han, for example, categorically denies the community value of social networks like Facebook. He defines its users as a "crowd" without unity, and "mass" without a common spirit. He compares each user on an online platform to the *hikikomori*, which are the pathologically isolated people who sit alone in a room in front of a computer screen: "Electronic media such as radio *assemble* human beings. In contrast, digital media *isolate* them."[14]

Günther Anders uses the expression "mass hermits" to refer to radio listeners, confirming how reductive a catastrophic approach to technological innovations is.

Whether Han likes it or not, when users publicly commemorate the deceased on their profile page, it is a specific collective ritual, more or less intentional and desired, with the following objectives: keeping that person's memory alive; resurrecting them spiritually through constant interaction between friends, acquaintances, and relatives; and creating a safe place in which those who are grieving feel protected. The message board of the deceased is filled with poignant messages, musical dedications, shared memories, or even just simple likes, hashtags, and tagging of other users to engage as many people as possible. Many direct messages are sent, attempts to extend communication beyond death. It's as if the loved one—now more than ever a digital ghost— could somehow read them and perhaps even respond, denying the separation between death and the image, which takes place during the burial of the corpse. Above the photograph of an acquaintance of mine who has died, a friend wrote: "Hang this up on the little cloud next to you. Happy Birthday!" Six years after his death, his friends and family continue to post pictures on his Facebook page quite frequently. Each time one of them posts, it creates an opportunity to communicate and feel connected to the group.

This specific collective ritual turns out to be surprisingly nuanced, confirming Hobbs and Burke's results, which describe a heterogeneous, complex landscape of connections between the living and the dead on Facebook. These collective rituals, or strategies for coping with loss, can be loosely divided into these five categories:

1. There are those who, mainly interested in creating a "group" to get past their own deeply personal pain, open a special page dedicated to the memory of the deceased. Each day users add memories and anecdotes about that person's past life to this page. This phenomenon is common around the world: the public page dedicated to the deceased, and managed by a chosen administrator, becomes an intimate and protected space in which many friends, who may live in different parts of the world, can find a safe place to work through their grief together. They freely express feelings that, due to shyness or modesty, they were unable to show when physically in front of one another. In this way they keep the memory of their mutual friend alive through sharing stories, images, and thoughts. Each participant thus broadens their knowledge of the deceased, who they may have known only for a short time or in a specific situation, and is able to feel less alone in their grief. Often, it's the partner of the deceased who feels the need to share memories of their lost loved one on a public page or on their own personal timeline.

The behavior of Marta Gaia, the girlfriend of Luca Varani—victim of one of Italy's most bizarre and horrific murders in recent years—is a classic example. For almost two years, Marta Gaia has shared memories devoted to her boyfriend, not on a special page, but on her own Facebook timeline with the privacy setting on "public." She tells funny stories about their life together and recreates special moments, for example, the celebration of both of their birthdays. Every post gets hundreds of likes from people she knows, but also from complete strangers, many of whom comment to be supportive of her. One day the caption on a photograph showing the couple together emphasized how unbearable her loss was and mentioned the terrible emptiness she felt because of his absence. According to Marta Gaia, the only way to ease this pain was to write about him, sharing those words with as many people as possible. Now just think, on this same social network, only a few "virtual" steps away, is the memorialized profile of one of Luca Varani's killers, who later committed suicide in prison.

Several digital death scholars highlight how behavior like that of Luca Varani's girlfriend, and of others who open public pages dedicated to the dearly departed, make it possible for the personality of the deceased to evolve rather than simply remaining static. That evolution—which, I emphasize, has nothing to do with the automation of chatbots, Counterparts, and holograms—happens through the progressive construction of an intersubjective collective memory, built from individual memories and different memorial events for the departed. This building starts with the opportunities offered by the transformation of every social network user into the message that they communicate and convey to others. This intersubjective collective memory creates a real virtual home for the community of the bereaved, composed of individual commemorations, from which the narrative and consolatory potential of social networks are derived.[15]

So it's no surprise that, as an alternative to Facebook, other digital platforms, primarily focused on the relationship between the bereaved and the dearly departed, are starting to spring up. One example among many is LifeVU (https://life -vu.com/), which has a particularly evocative slogan: "Reconnecting the Disconnected." LifeVU offers the deceased's friends and family members the opportunity to share experiences, stories, pictures, and special moments lived with that individual so that an online funerary memorial is created that *reconnects* a person who is no longer able to do so on their own. If death is *the* end of life, and not simply the end of *an* individual, the reconnection of the deceased with life through memory is a way to emphasize the natural bond between living and dying.

2. Some people also discover, through Facebook, that someone they once cared for a long time ago but have not seen in a long time has died. If it were not for the information made available through social networks, they might have tried to contact that person by mail or telephone and, receiving no response, have thought that person was intentionally ignoring them because they did not want to renew the friendship.

3. There are those who, having established a relationship in a digital environment through written exchanges with a person they have never met or spoken to, still feel real grief for the death of that person even if they are "only" virtual friends. This epistolary situation highlights the ability of social networks to generate feelings and emotions, for the most part authentic, among people who, having common tastes and ideas, perceive some form of bond between them. And they cultivate this bond without needing to

physically meet. This leaves the creation of a bond to their imaginations—a bond that then takes on a specific significance for the physical and psychological wellbeing of both individuals. On this topic Hans Belting argues that new media are likely to create "fellow travelers in imagination," each one sitting at home alone in front of their computers and sharing a communal "nowhere" that blends the illusion of reality with the importance of a dialogue's content, regardless of who is producing it.[16] The death of one of the two participants in this interaction is therefore comparable to the death of a friend or a loved one. Publicly showing one's grief in the virtual space, where the relationship was initiated and developed, is just as important and meaningful as it would be for a flesh-and-blood friend or relative. If what matters on social networks is the message, the content, rather than a physical presence, ultimately that means that death in the context of a relationship that is entirely virtual coincides with the end of that message. Projects like Eugenia Kuyda's Replika or, in the realm of Hollywood fantasy, Samantha in *Her* are based on the mechanism that regulates this kind of relationship on social media. The difference is that these projects intend to artificially create the interlocutor, without needing an actual human being behind the computer screen.

4. Then there are public commemorations for people who died after meticulously recounting, on their Facebook profiles, a personal battle with a fatal disease. Although these people are not personal friends, the power of their testimony should not be underestimated. A case in point is that of Giorgia Libero, a twenty-three-year-old Italian woman from

the city of Padua who gave a day-by-day account of her battle with lymphoma. She shared photographs of her medical
records on Facebook and Instagram. She posted selfies while
recovering in the hematology and immunology ward of
Padua's hospital. Over the course of two years she expressed
her hopes, her fears, and her despair. Scrolling through her
timeline, we can see a picture of her together with her dog
on the day the doctors advised her to send him away. Sharing this sad news with the public gave her the strength to
overcome her momentary disappointment. Then we see a
post where she expresses her joy when the doctors tell her
that her tumor is shrinking. Each one of her public posts
was read and commented on by hundreds, sometimes even
thousands, of people who sent her their virtual support.
Hundreds of likes for every single post up until the moment
when, on the August 18, 2016, her boyfriend communicated
the news of her death. Even today her Facebook profile, now
memorialized, is available as a public testimony to her struggle from the beginning up until her last breath. Her story
ended up being covered by all of Italy's major newspapers
and TV news programs. When her boyfriend posted a picture of Georgia on the anniversary of her death, it received
thousands of likes within the first few minutes.

From an emotional and psychological perspective, this
young woman's memorialized profile is unsettling. It is
yet another pitiless and, at the same time, vital description
of how death and disease come into a person's life. It also
underscores different elements that reveal the positive role
social networks can play when it comes to disease and death.

For those who, like Giorgia Libero, have to fight a terminal illness every single day, the ability to publicly talk about their physical hardships, hopes, fears, and emotions—together with texts, images, and video—makes it possible to avoid the circumstances in which Leo Tolstoy's protagonist finds himself in *The Death of Ivan Ilyich*, which even today still accurately represents the attitudes of contemporary society toward illness. When he is diagnosed with a terminal disease, Ivan Ilyich suffers isolation and the loss of public identity in a society that puts performance, perfection, and social standing above all else. He finds himself imprisoned in an insular bubble, which nobody has the time or the inclination to break through. This isolation is compounded by the way that society sees a tumor as a "macabre" subject. Here we think again about the saying "stroncato da un male incurabile" (struck down by an incurable disease), mentioned in the introduction to this book, which is used to avoid saying the words "cancer" and "death." The tumor is not perceived as what it is, which is to say a completely natural though sad circumstance, which could happen to anyone; but rather as a kind of judgment for a moral fault that is being visited upon the one who is ill. "Death is the inhuman conceptual excess," writes Rosi Braidotti, "the unrepresentable, unthinkable, unproductive black hole that we all fear."[17] This also translates into the distance we place between the sick and ourselves.

So giving a blow-by-blow account of every aspect of an illness in the context of one's own interactive virtual home, in which narrator and narrated are one and the same, is a way to shake off the emotional weight and "normalize" the situation, taking refuge in a personal safety net together with those who have lived or are living through the same experience. Turning the pain into a theatrical performance by sharing it can only help. And the hundreds of likes, shares, and supportive comments compensate, at least in part, for the daily suffering endured. Finally, recounting the course of the illness on a daily basis gives the sick person the sensation that they are being useful to others, laying the foundation for a story where the subject and the object of the narrative will live forever.

For those who participate as spectators in a story like Giorgia's, it offers them an opportunity to share their experiences, then to form a group and to rethink the natural role that death and disease play in life. While off-line it may be considered taboo to discuss this kind of topic, online it's possible to do so freely, diminishing anxieties and fears that, in most cases, are produced by repression and denial.

5. Finally, there are those instances in which public mourning on Facebook eventually drives the community created around a person's death to come up with new ideas and new spaces for coming together and dealing with the suffering linked to their common loss. There are many examples of blogs and websites created specifically for sharing experiences related to grief and mourning. One of these websites created in Italy is called *Soli ma insieme. Un sito per bambini e ragazzi in lutto* (Alone but together. A website for children and young people who are grieving). The site (http://solomainsieme.it)

was created by two nonprofit organizations working together. This is one of the first Italian websites that focuses on grieving children and adolescents and, consequently, it's also designed to help the adults—family members and teachers—who are with them in this traumatic moment in their lives. The basic idea of the site is to take the work done by the two organizations, associated with the Italian *Auto Mutuo Aiuto* (Mutual Self Help) groups that offer support for those coping with grief, and extend it to the internet. Projects like this once again demonstrate how the online dimension can have a positive influence on the off-line world, having an effect on their mutual integration.

RIP: Social Networks and the Death of Celebrities

The study by Hobbs and Burke also sheds light on the existence of a safety net that coalesces around the death of a person and provides the necessary coping tools for those who feel that their grief is not acknowledged. Unacknowledged bereavement happens when there are losses for which people don't feel free to express their suffering because they think it will not be understood by society and institutions. For example, consider the grief experienced when a pet, to which someone is deeply attached, or a particularly admired and idealized celebrity dies.

Commemoration of deceased celebrities on social media is widespread and emblematic of the schizophrenic link between death and digital culture. Over the years, Facebook,

Twitter, and Instagram have been loaded with expressions of grief and condolence posted by users whenever a star dies. From David Bowie to George Michael, Robin Williams, Dolores O'Riordan, Philip Seymour Hoffman, and Chris Cornell: an uninterrupted flood of posts, tweets, photos, videos, and various testimonials are put forward to publicly express the importance that artist had in the social and cultural life of individuals. The phenomenon has become so ordinary that news of a celebrity death on any given day is placed at the top of that star's official Twitter or Facebook page even before it reaches the news outlets. It's certainly not unusual for social media memorials to be published even before the death has been officially announced. Tom Petty's death is a perfect example. *Rolling Stone* magazine rashly spread the news of his death without making sure that he had actually died. Consequently, the newsfeeds of the singer's fans and of music aficionados in general began to fill up with condolence messages and video dedications while the American singer was still fighting for his life, even if he was in critical condition. Even before he died, the name "Petty" topped the lists of trending topics and views of his famous song "Learning to Fly" on YouTube, with the accompanying surge of sharing on social media, went up by 200 percent compared to the previous days. Petty's daughter, Annakim Violette, had harsh words for *Rolling Stone*—delivered, of course, via a public post on Instagram.

Every time a famous musician, actor, writer, or sports figure dies, social media users compete to see who can write the most poignant message, or share the most iconic images, video clips, and quotes from that celebrity's career. There are those who sadly tell the story of why and for how many years they had admired that particular artist. Sometimes the sole aim is getting as many likes as possible. Then there are those who replace their own profile pictures with that of the deceased, those who claim to have known them, those who analyze the celebrity's artistic production arguing that it has either been undervalued or overrated—followed by all of the related discussions and disputes. Some disagree with the practice of publicly assessing the work of the artist on social media in the immediate aftermath of their death, out of respect for their mourning loved ones. There are others still who argue that the gravity of death itself is undermined when a user's seemingly earnest commemorative post is followed by another post showing what they ate for lunch that day.

The death of a celebrity creates a tragicomic agglomeration of memorials on social media that includes celebrations of that person's life and work, along with arguments, narcissisms, and real expressions of grief. This "visual" presence of death distorts people's emotions, sometimes degenerating into a kind of digital necrophilia. A case in point is that of Canadian porn star August Ames who was "cyberbullied" while she was alive as a result of some homophobic comments that she posted on Twitter. Following her suicide in 2017, her reputation was rehabilitated to the point where she received a number of posthumous award nominations, including one for Female Performer of the Year from AVN (Adult Video News) in 2018. Public exonerations, compulsive internet searches of her name, and views of videos in which she starred quadrupled—and everywhere comments were left, full of condolences and memorials: *Eros* and *Thanatos*, literally.

On this topic I would like to share the words of Giovanni Ziccardi, who argues that we should not necessarily dismiss this type of over-the-top public commemoration. In fact, in a certain way, it represents "an act that *democratizes* death, turning the deceased into a 'trending' personality in the digital environment."[18] Indeed, the nature of social networks is that of being "immediate, characterized by impulses and always changing." In addition, although it is plausible to think that these people have little interest in the artist and that their only real interest is in "participating" and "being present," narcissistically focusing attention on themselves, it can be said that even a superficial celebration of an artist's life can mask deeper feelings and helpful insights that could lead to more serious reflection. "Often," Ziccardi observes, "the fans of a singer or actor constitute a 'family' who feel a common bond among themselves, and social networks become the best way to share what is a tangible fact, what is real even if it is on the internet."[19] Along these same lines, consider collective participation in the funeral of a famous person. It's now established practice to go to a celebrity's funeral or memorial service; no one talks about the reasons for doing so. Some go so that they can say that they were there, others because they are curious and want to share the gossip with their friends and relatives. Still others go to symbolically express how important that person was to them. The same thing happens in commemorations posted on social media. And although it may seem strange when someone shares a picture of the pizza they've just eaten right after posting a commemorative message, we should remember how people sometimes behave at a friend's funeral. Someone might tell a funny joke or an off-color story. Real life is, after all, a mix of solemnity and comedy.

The death of a famous person can offer the opportunity, on social media, to initiate discussions that are objectively useful. For example, because he suffered from depression, the suicide of singer Chris Cornell generated a lot of conversation about depression and about suicide prevention strategies that could be implemented off-line. Lastly, there are cases like that of Lemmy Kilmister, front man for the British heavy metal band Motörhead, whose funeral was livestreamed on YouTube, watched by millions of users around the world. These fans then exchanged condolences among themselves on Facebook.

Superficial or not, this type of public commemoration makes the need for a collective grieving process evident. Mourning has been confined to the private sphere, far from the public eye, for too many years. The label of grief and mourning itself imposes the obligation to suffer alone and in private—specifically, in your own home and not in public spaces in which people gather. We must overcome our grief as soon as possible, return to work immediately, and make no public show of our fragility in shared spaces. The

result of these tacit expectations is that those who are grieving feel disoriented, left to fend for themselves, and crushed
by external social pressure.

Social networks offer an alternative, or at least a starting
point for rethinking and changing the essential elements in
how individuals experience the grieving process. If what is
important for those who have suffered a loss is recovering
a healthy balance in their own lives, then expressing their
grief and pain on Facebook and receiving a meaningful,
supportive response may well be one of the many avenues
worth pursuing. As Jan Assmann reminds us, memorializing
the dead is "a paradigmatic way of 'establishing the community,'" because reflecting on the link with them consolidates
one's own identity. [20] Thus, cases in which the commemoration involves a celebrity can become a model for rediscover-
ing the sense of community within our public spaces and
more effectively integrating our fragile lives into the broader
circle of existence.

Digital Testimonials and Cremations: Social Network Rules

The relationship between social networks and death, in
addition to the many questions we've already discussed,
brings the issue of personal privacy to the forefront. There
are often discrepancies between the desires of the deceased
individual, those of their various family members, and the
rules established by social networks. Several cases have been

reported that highlight just how sensitive an issue a user's postmortem online presence is when it comes to interactive digital platforms. For example, in 2014, the relatives and friends of Harry Friar (who had died the year before) received Facebook "friend requests" from an unknown person who had opened an account in the name of the deceased, appropriating his identity and images. Obviously, this was deeply shocking for those who had suffered through Friar's loss, and they immediately turned to the appropriate authorities to try to identify the culprit. More recently, in Italy, public attention was captured by the situation surrounding Luca Borgoni, a twenty-two-year-old who died in an accident during a trip to the mountains on July 8, 2017. His mother, Cristina Giordana—with the help of her daughter and *without* her son's *prior consent*—figured out Luca's Facebook password and, for months, wrote first-person posts (with the privacy setting on "public") as if it were her son, Luca himself, still writing. One of the public posts that the mother wrote, identifying herself as her son, said: "It's going to be Christmas in a few days. ... I have to come up with some way to make it less sad for my parents and my sister Giulia. This is the first year that neither I, nor my beloved grandmother Rosangela, will be physically present." Despite the fact that it was just writing and that the mother felt the need to process her intense grief over the loss of her son by giving Luca a voice, someone notified Facebook of his death. The account was immediately changed to a memorialized profile, preventing the mother from logging in and impersonating her son. The mother protested and, more importantly, asked why she could inherit the house and the bank account of her dead son, but not his Facebook profile. Giordana argued that there was nothing wrong with "keeping him alive" on social media.[21] A few years earlier, in 2012, something similar happened in the United States. When Becky Palmer died from a brain tumor at the age of nineteen, her mother Louise had no way to access her daughter's account because the account had been automatically memorialized. Previously, the mother had found some solace in reading her daughter's private messages from time to time.

The conflict of interest between personal privacy and digital inheritance on Facebook took center stage in a court battle in Berlin that lasted for more than five years. In 2012 a fifteen-year-old girl died after she was struck by a subway train, having fallen on the rails. Her parents asked Facebook for access to her account and her private messages in order to determine whether she might have committed suicide or been the victim of bullies. When she was fourteen, the girl had given her Facebook username and password to her mother. However, once her friends informed Facebook of her death, they immediately memorialized her account and her mother was denied access. While anyone who went to her page could still see the photos and posts she shared when she was alive, it was no longer possible to log in to her account. Requests for access by her parents were rejected in order to maintain the young woman's privacy. Her parents did not give up and took the case to Berlin's courts. After five years of rulings and appeals, in 2017 an appeals court ruled in favor of Facebook, denying the parents the right to access their deceased daughter's private conversations. At that time, Facebook expressed understanding of the parents' position and promised to work to find a future solution that would balance their users' need for privacy with the needs of the family and friends of the deceased in cases such as this one. That ruling was appealed and overturned in mid-2018 by Germany's Federal Court of Justice.

We can find ample food for thought in these examples, which are hardly isolated cases. First, international law has not yet been able to provide satisfactory answers to the needs of the bereaved. Access to the personal data stored online by people who have died is only guaranteed to those who are acting in the interest of protecting the deceased or for family reasons that deserve protection. But no accurate indication is given regarding which interests need to be safeguarded and what "family reasons" deserve protection. Second, Facebook and other social networks have decided to give precedence to protecting the personal privacy and the private conduct of their individual users over any other considerations.

The case of Luca Borgoni is a perfect example: since the young man had not left any specific instructions, it was not possible to objectively establish whether or not his mother's desire to enter his "virtual home," giving her deceased son an active voice through her own words, were in conflict with his wishes. Perhaps the young man would never have wanted his mother to start writing in his name after his death, publishing posts that bore the official digital signature of "Luca Borgoni." Moreover, it is certainly not a given that what made the mother feel better was also beneficial to others who were suffering from his loss. It may have induced pain and anguish in some people to see a Facebook post written as if Luca *were* still alive. The point is still the same: in the virtual environment of a social network, the disembodied subject is transformed into the message that is shared and communicated to others. The subject is completely identified with the message. Therefore, the message is never neutral, because it coalesces with an individual identity. Luca's mother by proxy became the digital ghost of her son. From a certain perspective, she was unwittingly doing the same thing with her son that James Vlahos consciously did with his father in creating a chatbot. The difference was that the woman had taken upon herself a role that was not hers to play, certainly not in the context of a memory box of stories such as Facebook.

The Berlin case is more sensitive, since the teenager's parents were motivated by the need to know if her death was an accident or a suicide. All the same, without prior written consent from the interested party, gaining access to her private conversations constitutes a gray area because it also involves the privacy of those with whom she interacted. Again, their teenage daughter might have been perfectly happy for her parents to look through her chats, and the only opinion that really counts is hers.

These cases are only the tip of the iceberg when it comes to dealing with the concrete issues that follow the death of social network users, and they highlight a widespread lack of end-of-life preparation in the digital environment. That is why it's important to be well aware of the various social network's rules about what happens when a user dies. Knowing a social network's parameters makes it easier to avoid possible misunderstandings.

Facebook

Over the years, Facebook's administrators have been trying to understand how best to help those who have suffered bereavement. The first issues that they have confronted are the problematic nature of birthday notifications for someone who has died (as these tend to reopen the wound inflicted by loss) and the fact that the relatives of the deceased do not all want the same thing. Often there are situations in which some relatives would like to delete the account while others want to keep it active. This kind of disagreement happens in situations where the owner of the account has left no clear instructions. This is why Facebook has established some rules that allow each individual user to leave clear information about what they would like done with their online profile after they die. The wishes expressed by the user are final and take precedence over any desire expressed by friends and family. This is why everyone who makes use of social networks is strongly advised to make their personal choices about the fate of their account well in advance, in order to avoid the unpleasant situations described in this chapter. In other words, it would be advisable to make what might be considered a "digital will."

To make sure that, once you have died, your account will not appear in ads, People You May Know suggestions, and birthday reminders, you can decide in advance to

"memorialize" your account following your death. Memorializing an account means that once the social network's
administrators have been sent a death certificate, a copy of
the obituary, or a notarized statement, the word "Remembering" will be shown next to the person's name on their
profile, followed by this phrase: "We hope people who love
(deceased user's name) will find comfort in visiting his/her
profile to remember and celebrate his/her life." In this way,
all of that user's "friends" will be aware that they have died
and, depending on the privacy settings of the account,
they will be able to share memories on the memorialized
timeline. Content the person shared during their lifetime
remains visible with its original privacy settings. However,
no one can log in to a memorialized account and make any
changes.

The only person who can take action is known as the
"legacy contact," someone who was chosen in advance to
look after the account once it becomes memorialized. The
legacy contact, who must be a legal adult, can write a pinned
post for the deceased user's profile, respond to new friend
requests, and update the profile picture. They cannot create
posts in the name of the deceased, read private messages,
or remove friends. The legacy contact can also download a
copy of what the user has shared over the years, like photos, videos and wall posts, profile and contact information,
events, and a friends list. This way they can create a type of
digital memory box for that person, which contains the stories they've told over the years. The legacy contact will not
receive messages, advertisements on which the deceased had

clicked, or information about security and settings. Facebook states that it may add additional capabilities for legacy contacts in the future.

Clearly, users can also choose to leave the account as is after they die, or have it deleted permanently.

In the first case, the user gives no instructions in advance and does not prepare a digital will. This is problematic because the user's profile will, if no friend or family member informs the social network of their death, continue to "wander" in a ghostly way among the timelines of the living, receiving friend requests and birthday greetings; they may still be tagged and invited to public events or asked to "like" pages for companies and products. A failure to officially inform Facebook of a user's death means that family members or friends who know that person's username and password can log in and enter the "virtual home" of the deceased, just like Luca Borgoni's mother. On the contrary, if someone notifies the company of the user's death, their profile is automatically memorialized.

In the second case, at the same time that the corpse is permanently removed from the world of the living, the deceased person's Facebook profile undergoes a kind of *digital cremation*. If the account owner has given prior instructions for deletion, the digital cremation will happen as soon as an official document confirming their death is received. As the physical body is removed, so is the digital one. The "digital ashes" are kept only by those who have downloaded the images, posts, and status updates of the deceased prior to notifying the social network of their death.

Noting a steady increase in the number of deceased users' profiles, in early 2019 Facebook decided to offer some new features. In particular they are rolling out a new Tributes section for memorialized profiles. This special space offers a place to say goodbye and otherwise honor the memory of users who have chosen to memorialize their profiles and named a legacy contact in advance. Tributes will appear under a separate tab on the official memorialized profile, preserving the original timeline of the deceased while offing a special place where friends and family can share commemorative messages, photos, and videos. For example, on that person's birthday, messages and memories posted by their contacts will appear in the Tributes section. The legacy contact will be able to control the content posted within it, limiting access to a specific audience, eliminating posts considered inappropriate as well as any tags deemed disrespectful. In other words, the Tributes tab will become the area dedicated to the memory of a deceased loved one.

In addition, to help families when a user hasn't chosen to have their account memorialized, Facebook will use algorithms to keep inappropriate notifications from appearing. Finally, although minors cannot choose a legacy contact, their parents will now be able to ask permission to manage those accounts if their child has died.

Twitter, LinkedIn, Snapchat, and Tumblr

When it comes to privacy and digital inheritance, these companies are very limited and strict. When an account holder dies, the only option for friends and relatives is to deactivate the account. An authorized person fills out the appropriate form, notifying the company of the user's death, and sends it, along with multiple copies of the death certificate, all the necessary information about the deceased, and copies of their identity documents, to the social network concerned. After they have fully reviewed the information, the administrators delete the user's profile. The person who has died in the real world off-line also dies in the online world. No third parties are allowed access to the deceased user's private account. Digital cremation is the only option. Twitter has a specific page (https://help.twitter.com/forms/privacy) where the company offers the following option: "I want to request the deactivation of a deceased or incapacitated person's account," which you can select to receive all of the necessary information.

Instagram

This social network allows an immediate family member of the deceased to choose between memorializing the account or deleting it. If the first option is chosen, once Instagram has received all of the required documents and certificates, the account of the deceased is memorialized and no third parties can access it in any way. What is interesting is how Instagram's policies reflect the unwritten sociocultural practices regarding the erasure of death from everyday life. Memorialized profiles are, in a way, isolated from those of the living as well as from the search engines and updating systems. In addition, comments, photographs, followers, likes, and privacy settings cannot be changed. Instagram's

administrators say this is for reasons of privacy and deco-
rum. If a user or an immediate family member prefers to
have the account deleted, the appropriate documentation
certifying the account holder's death must be sent to Instagram. Because this social network does not currently allow
users to download their content directly, it is advisable to
save the photographs posted to the account to some other
digital media. This can be done via a free service, like Insta-
port.me, so that they will be available to third parties when
the account holder is no longer alive.

Google

Google offers a more nuanced solution. The user first goes to
the page where they can manage the settings for an inactive
account (https://myaccount.google.com/u/0/inactive) and
establishes a plan for how their account will be managed
in case of death or if they simply stop using their Google
account. It's possible to choose up to ten executors, who will
decide the fate of an inactive account and will, if they have
been given them explicit permission to do so, have access to
all of the deceased person's information, including emails,
photos, and documents stored in the cloud.

A user may decide to have their account deleted upon
their death. They can also choose to have it stored and maintained by the people they have selected, who must show the
appropriate death certificates in order to access the account.

If no activity has been detected on the account for an
extended period of time, Google will make an effort to find
out if the account holder is alive or dead—namely, if that

person is still interested in utilizing its services or not. So on the basis of the instructions it has previously received, Google will try to contact the user via email or text message (providing a telephone number or that of a trusted contact is mandatory). The period of inactivity that passes before Google takes action is up to the individual user, and it can be from three to eighteen months.

As Ziccardi points out, the deletion of a Google account implies the elimination of a broad range of personal data: "Today, a Google profile has become a hub for dozens of services such as e-mail addresses, groups, pages, video collections, data stored in the cloud via Google Drive and more. This means that the 'death' of an account brings on a chain reaction involving other linked accounts and services that can suddenly no longer be accessed."[22] You should keep this in mind so that you can make the appropriate decision.

The difficulties associated with managing your own digital legacy can seem overwhelming; for this very reason many services have been established to help individual social network users. One of these is DeadSocial (http://deadsocial .org), which offers the tools necessary for building your own digital legacy in an informed way. First of all, it provides a comprehensive guide of what is available, in case of death, from Facebook, Twitter, Instagram, LinkedIn, Google, and various blogs. In addition, DeadSocial has a series of tools and methods for arranging your final digital wishes, for planning the end of your online life, and for organizing your off-line funeral. Then there are services, like Entruster or Legacy Locker, that safeguard the access codes to your online accounts and pass them on to your chosen beneficiaries. However, these services are not yet operating on the basis of specific legal directives.

Deathswitch, a company that shut down in late 2015, was focused on the unintended damage that an unexpected death could cause in terms of both the private and the work-related content of our email. Death suddenly takes away a lifetime of passwords and log-in information, leaving coworkers and friends with no ability to access the deceased person's work-related files unless they had been using a Cloud Storage service to share their work in progress. Death-switch's task was to automatically send out predetermined information to other people who had been specifically chosen by the user in advance, upon that user's death. This made it possible to compose emails with specific content to be sent out, after the fact, to relatives, friends, coworkers and—sure—even enemies. What made Deathswitch a bit bizarre was its method for confirming that a user was still alive. The service regularly sent out an email with the following question: "Are you alive?" If, after several attempts, the service did not receive a reply, the system automatically activated, assuming that the account holder was deceased. Who knows if the failure of Deathswitch was linked to the account holder's misunderstanding of the question and subsequent emailing of personal data to the account holder's contacts.

3
Digital Inheritance and Hi-Tech Funeral Rites

The Continuous Bond: World Soul 2.0

The German designer Leoni Fischer, a product design student at Weimar's Bauhaus University, created the Necropolis project. This project was able to represent our digital existence on Facebook in a concrete, physical way. To keep the dead alive, maintaining their contact with us, Necropolis uses an algorithm to transform a person's Facebook activity into a postmortem memorial. The individual's data sets off a sequence of light signals, preserving the uniqueness of the individual, and of the relationship that has been severed, using tiny LED lights.

Fischer's artistic project is a further confirmation of how social networks are able to take on the traditional symbolic communication between the hereafter and the now, communication that is perceived—by the person in front of the computer screen—as reciprocal. It's worth noting that in international studies regarding digital death, terms like "interactive digital headstones," "techno-spirituality" and "digital soul" are commonly used to describe the relationship being created between Facebook and death. Metaphors such as digital ghosts, technological memory boxes, and digital doppelgängers work along the same lines.

However, it is important to highlight some of the psychological, philosophical, and literary references that—in emphasizing the links between the world of the living and the world of the dead brought about by social networks—take us in the direction of experiments, ideas, and inventions that further articulate the presence of the dead in the digital environment. From a psychological point of view, the recognition of symbolic communication between the hereafter and the now generated by social networks has something in common with the *continuing bonds* theory. This theory was set forth, primarily by Dennis Klass, Phyllis R. Silverman, and Steven Nickman, in their book *Continuing Bonds: New Understandings of Grief*, which challenged the established views expressed in contemporary studies on grief and mourning.[1] This theory links the healthy rebuilding of the bereaved person's life, following a painful loss, to the need to find a specific "place" for the deceased in their life as it continues. This "place" is closely associated with the *memory* the bereaved has of the deceased, a continuing bond that is often experienced in ways that include

1. an awareness of the persistent presence of the deceased in one's life (note that this is a *symbolic* presence, typical of those who feel that, when their loved one was alive, they had a decisive influence on their lives and development);

2. an internal dialogue *with* the deceased, usually when standing at a graveside or while looking at a photograph, during which the need to talk about your own emotions and to seek spiritual support in moments of difficulty or success is united with the objective awareness of that person's irrevocable physical absence; and

3. talking *about* the deceased in public, so that the bereaved reconstructs a new narrative for their own life, which serves as the foundation for their future.

Undoubtedly, social networks, and Facebook in particular, provide the tools required to implement this kind of continuing bond between the living and the dead. They meet the criteria of these three processes, as evidenced by both the narrative histories that form once an individual user dies and by Hobbs and Burke's study of the grieving process.

From a philosophical perspective, there is a specific application within the digital realm of the concept of *anima mundi* or *world soul* (*Weltseele*), a term nineteenth-century German Romantic philosophy used to describe the relationship between the living and the dead and the reciprocal correspondence between the natural (*Naturphilosophie*) and the spirit world (*Geisterwelt*) within a pantheistic and vitalistic conception of reality. In fact, the anima mundi supports the interconnection of all of the world's individual fragments (regardless of whether they are alive or dead), which make up the natural and spiritual totality of all things; each individual contributes to this world soul in a unique and distinctive way. Something similar is happening today in the infosphere where we are experiencing the shift from an individual identity to an intersubjective or interconnected one. This shift brings to light the original character of human identity, according to which all human beings are informational in themselves, part of a participatory universe, an All-One, actively embodying the dead, which is to say the presence of an absence.

In *The Little Book of Life after Death* (1836), Gustav Theodor Fechner argues that the meeting point between the living and the dead is memory and that the first holds the second, in the sense that "our memory of the dead is but a new consciousness, in retrospect, of the results of their known life here, yet the life on the other side will be led conformably to that in this world."[2] A bit later he adds that, in the same way that a physical blow is felt both by the giver and the receiver, when one remembers the dead it is a "shock of consciousness" experienced not only by the survivors but also by those who have died. The fact that those who are still alive don't physically "see" or "hear" the deceased's shock of consciousness doesn't mean that it isn't real.

This type of psychological and philosophical bond between the dead and the living forms the theoretical foundation of George Saunders's recent *Lincoln in the Bardo: A Novel*.[3] The novel uses the death of the Abraham Lincoln's beloved, eleven-year-old son Willie in 1862 as an opportunity to describe and tell the stories of the dead souls that populate the "bardo," a Tibetan Buddhist term for the intermediate, transitional state between a life that has ended and a rebirth into a future life. *The Tibetan Book of the Dead* explains how the bardo is a liminal phase in which the spirits' suffering results from the difficulty of accepting detachment from their earthly life, therefore from their loved ones. One of the fascinating aspects of Saunders's novel is how the polyphonic or multi-voiced monologues of the spirits who inhabit the bardo—similar to the multiple posts on a Facebook newsfeed—describe contradictory perspectives of reality, therefore the many worlds, existing and recreated by each of them, based on their individual, distinctive choices and communal dialogues. These monologues are continually interwoven with accounts of Lincoln's life and historical facts from that era. One of the most meaningful events in the novel is when Lincoln, in despair, visits the cemetery's crypt and embraces his son's corpse. Not surprisingly, he doesn't see Willie's *spirit*, which is outside the coffin, running to meet him, begging him to hug and caress *him*, not the lifeless body in the "sick-box." This is how the spirits refer to their coffins, as they are commenting to each other while watching the meeting between the president and his son. At a certain point, Willie's spirit goes back into the corpse in order to be closer to his father. Lincoln starts to cry as if he has sensed a change in the body he is clutching in his arms. As I mentioned, this scene in the novel is narrated through the dialogue of the other spirits of the dead, an exchange that brings to mind the kind of conversation and arguments typical of those on social networks.

The feeling of symbolically maintaining communication with those who have died by addressing them in a conversational way, as is possible on Facebook, coincides with

Fechner and Saunders's philosophical and literary descriptions. In other words, it seems as if the spirit of the deceased can somehow sense the words and actions expressed and that, if combined with the clear awareness of the definitive absence of the deceased, may help the bereaved overcome their suffering and find the motivation to rebuild their lives. This may explain, among other things, the increase in interactions on Facebook during a period of mourning.

With this in mind, I will now describe some of the methods used in the digital environment to keep communication between the living and the dead active. I will broaden the discussion regarding the link between social networks and death and highlight digital culture's vast potential when it comes to reimagining funeral celebrations and remembering the dead.

WhatsApp and Messaging the Dead

A dismayed Franz Kafka asked himself how humans could have invented an idea as unhealthy as that of staying in contact with each other through the exchange of letters. According to him, it was no better than writing to ghosts. Not only that, the letters' contents were then consumed by other voracious ghosts while in transit. "One can think about someone far away and one can hold on to someone nearby; everything else is beyond human power."[4] Kafka, who is talking about paper letters, was obviously unaware that one day people would be using messaging applications like WhatsApp, which intensify the ghostliness of written communication.

The relationship between death and grief and WhatsApp is just as complex as the relationship between death and grief and social networks. The dead haunt our WhatsApp contact lists. Their profiles, which include their photos and status posts, are mixed in with those of the still living, creating a situation where each individual, any time they scroll through their contacts list, finds themselves confronted with their deceased friends or loved ones—which is to say confronted with the incarnation of an absent presence. In the same way as a Facebook "memory" of a deceased friend provokes a sudden and unexpected reminder of death, the WhatsApp profile of a deceased friend becomes a kind of memorial shrine, offering up to us once again the photographs exchanged, the sound of that friend's voice in the voice messages sent, and all of the chat messages written over the years. The presence of the deceased on WhatsApp has an emotionally disruptive effect: this app is only used for private conversations, or those shared with a limited number of friends. The personal dimension of the relationship makes the person who is irrevocably lost seem even closer and more present.

This situation confronts us with some difficult questions: What should we do with the WhatsApp profile of a deceased contact? Delete it or keep it? Ziccardi, posing these questions to his "friends" on Facebook, noted that the majority of them were intent on keeping the profiles of those who had died in their WhatsApp contacts list. Even though a casual poll of Facebook friends has no statistical value, he came to the conclusion that, for many people, deleting a deceased person's profile was profoundly painful since it reiterated the physical reality of the death in the digital environment. In fact, keeping a person on one's contact list was seen as a sign of love and respect for the deceased and also a way of seeing them again, if just for an instant, reviving memories and joyful moments experienced together. That is to say, it is a way of keeping the memory of our loved one's tone of voice and way of expressing themselves alive over the course of time. All we have to do is listen to a few of their voice messages and reread the chats exchanged. "These elements become, in this way, an important part of our archive of memories and are integrated with that person's Facebook profile," observes Giovanni Ziccardi.[5] There are also those who believe that keeping a deceased person's profile on a contact list reopens wounds and risks pushing the grieving process in the wrong direction, creating distress and sadness. From that perspective, deleting a number from WhatsApp is like performing a healthy "digital cremation," after which the bereaved can begin to restart their lives anew.

An unusual situation exists regarding the link between WhatsApp and the dead: it's like sending a direct message to the deceased. A friend told me about the day she graduated from university seven months after her boyfriend had died. As soon as she received her official diploma, her first instinct was to pick up her smartphone and send a WhatsApp message to him and let him know her happy news. This situation is actually more common than most people realize and warrants further exploration.

First of all, sending a WhatsApp message to someone who has died is nothing like making public posts on Facebook. As expressions of grief, Facebooks posts serve a useful purpose because, despite being ostensibly directed to the dearly departed, they are also read and shared with other bereaved users. On Facebook, a communal theatricality is part and parcel of the communication with the dead.

In contrast, a direct message to the deceased on WhatsApp is a *private*, confidential message that is literally "sent." My friend sent her own important news directly to her boyfriend who was no longer alive. She sent it to him, to him alone and no one else. This message could only be read by the living person who wrote it and, *hypothetically*, by the dead person who received it. From the moment the send button is tapped, the sender may be hoping to see the double check mark to indicate that the message was delivered, followed by the moment when those two gray check marks turn blue to indicate that the message has been read. But, aside from such hope, this is a definite, intentional, *symbolic gesture*, seemingly irrational and in contradiction to reality: the desire to communicate her happy news—her graduation—to the person with whom she most wanted to share it.

And so WhatsApp, if used in a symbolic way, with a clear awareness of the reality of death, can become a romantic link between the departed and the one who has been left behind. It can be a way of keeping the bond alive in the mind and emotions of the living. We should not underestimate the symbolic and romantic significance of this gesture. It is a very concrete way of expressing those continuing bonds between the hereafter and the now. We have a digital *body* to contain the *spirit* of each individual, whether they are alive or dead. The fact remains that the person who sent the message will only see the one gray check mark, no confirmation of receipt will come. This could be a healthy way to come to terms with how things are now and with the fact that they will never go back to how they were before. Life goes on, so to take a moment to symbolically recover the lost intimacy with a loved one can be healthy. Obviously, what is important is that this moment is understood and performed as a symbolic action within the context of a clear and resolute awareness of death.

Direct messages to the deceased via WhatsApp also help us clearly understand the reasons behind the invention of chatbots and projects like Eter9, Eterni.me, and LifeNaut. As soon as the message is sent, it's immediately followed by the uncontrollable desire to receive one more time, *at least once*, a reply. Remember Ash's joy in "Be Right Back," when he found out that he was *going to be* a father after Martha told him she was pregnant? These inventions are responding to this desire and are trying to satisfy it. They are also working from the sure knowledge that we—be it on WhatsApp or in any other interactive environment on the internet—reproduce ourselves with an immeasurable quantity of personal material, which will define our profile forever.

This awareness, beyond the experiments on digital immortality and keeping in mind the precious personal resources contained in WhatsApp chats, compels us to reflect on the meaning of our digital legacies and the consequences of those legacies in the context of the continuing bond with our deceased loved ones and the different ways of dealing with funerals.[6]

An Indelible Impression on the Internet

According to Adam Ostrow, former editor in chief of *Mashable*, one of the world's most popular blogs, forty-eight hours of video are being uploaded to YouTube every single minute, two hundred million Tweets are being posted to Twitter every day, and the average Facebook user is creating ninety pieces of content each month.[7] This vast quantity of images, video, and written material, which accumulates and is constantly shared and often virally re-shared on social networks, is always associated with an email address, without which it's difficult or even impossible to register on a social network.

Every email address, first and foremost, functions as a container for the private and work correspondence that each one of us has accumulated over the last several decades, starting at the birth of the internet. Consider the thousands of emails, including love letters and private arguments, as well as a substantial amount of work-related activities and data both private and publicly available. These email addresses are connected to hundreds of other accounts, each associated with a user name, a password, the terms of service, and a privacy policy. These accounts, in addition to the social networks, cloud storage services, and mobile messaging services already mentioned, are also linked to virtual locations that are further afield. There are online stores (Amazon, eBay, etc.), search engines and web portals for travel, vacations, restaurants, car rentals, tourist attractions (TripAdvisor, eDreams, Booking.com, etc.); then there are personal blogs on WordPress, music libraries and playlists (iTunes, Spotify, etc.), national and international libraries, dating sites, home banking, online supermarkets, and so on. Signing up for each one of these accounts implies the widespread and often unintended distribution of one's personal data to hundreds of companies, agencies, and service providers. Your telephone number, your social-security number, your credit card information, various photographs, a history of the sites you've visited, and the cookies that advertisers have tagged you with are all circulating serenely around the internet.

The internet is so obsessed with archiving that a music fan can create a personal profile on a site like setlist.fm (https://www.setlist.fm). On this website, users from around the globe are engaging in a meticulous collaborative effort to compile the setlists (documents listing all the songs a band intends to play during a given performance) of all of the concerts in the world. Each user creates a personal profile in which they keep an archive of the concerts that they have personally attended. Each concert is connected to a web page that shows its setlist. In a less specialized area, the Internet Archive (https://archive.org) has built a digital library of websites and their content so that researchers, historians, and scholars have access to an endless amount of material from which they can derive an authentic archaeology of the web. Among the various sections of the Internet Archive is the Wayback Machine (https://archive.org/web/), which makes it possible to find websites that are no longer currently online. It's also possible to find versions of the same website from different years in order to see how it has changed over time.

The digital environment is adept at making us think about time, which is progressively distributed in a fragmentary way on the surface of our screens, in spatial terms. This spatialization of time ensures that nothing disappears from the Internet, remaining available to posterity even when it seems to be lost. The "perfect crime" that Baudrillard talks about in terms of television is accomplished through "an unconditional realization of the world by the actualization of all data, the transformation of all our acts and all events into pure information," so that the world will reach a "final solution" sooner than anticipated through the meticulous cloning of reality.[8]

Now let's take a moment and try to grasp all of the traces left by our own online presence, taking account of all of our activities, the distribution of our data, and the general archiving mania of the Internet. Let's try to do it, knowing that every trace, more often than not, exists in tandem with other users, in a vast digital environment of interconnected identities. Already we have found ourselves in a universe of memories and personal information, with indefinable boundaries, almost impossible to navigate. In fact, the individual user is often unaware of all of the traces they have left on various websites and all the accounts they have opened in their lifetimes. If it is unlikely that we will remember all the passwords we have ever created; certainly it is impossible to remember the terms of service and privacy policies to which we have agreed, which has permitted the sending of our personal data to third parties.

Ultimately, there is no way to plan and execute your own "digital death" despite the existence of targeted services such as Deseatme (https://www.deseat.me/) and Just Delete Me (http://backgroundchecks.org/justdeleteme/). Companies like this are working to help users delete all their accounts, one by one; however, as they are doing this work, they receive in exchange a precise digital map of that person's digital identity and thus all of their movements online. And so we find ourselves back where we started.

Planning for the "death" of our data, digital objects, and information—to coincide with our own physical death—is even more problematic. Back in 2011 there was quite a stir when scientific journalist Derek K. Miller asked his family to publish a prepared blog post immediately following his death from cancer. In this lengthy post he said his goodbyes to his loved ones and his readers. Miller defined this post as the first part of the process of turning his active website into an archive. Unlike Miller, most people don't give much thought to the postmortem destiny of their digital homes. Much like how many put off thinking about death off-line as well. One wonders how many impersonal funerals, or disputes about what to do with physical assets, are the result of a family's reluctance to talk to their loved ones about how they would like to be remembered, or how they would like their possessions handled. It's no wonder that the Swedish practice of "death cleaning" is currently so popular.

If the organization of one's physical possessions is apt to be cursorily managed, just imagine how the digital ones fare! These digital possessions are stored online but often off-line as well, and they include everything that is in our computers, smartphones, or tablets (eReader, music, and media collections on Windows Media Player, and the list goes on). We have already partially addressed the difficulties that come up on social networks when a user has not left a digital will to regulate how to deal with the content they shared in that context. Now we can broaden the discussion further to what is commonly called *digital inheritance*, which touches the lives of an increasingly large number of people as we get further away from the birth of the internet. As Derrida wrote, "Inheritance is never a *given*, it is always a task" and "That we *are* heirs does not mean that we *have* or that we *receive* this or that, some inheritance that enriches us one day with this or that, but that the *being* of what we are is first of all inheritance, whether we like it or know it or not."[9] And the urgency of taking on this task is underlined by the evidence that the dead continue to live symbolically in the hereafter only as long as the living remember them. They disappear once the last living person who knew them during their lifetime dies.

Digital Inheritance

Now that it's clear that you need to carefully consider your digital legacy, let's stop and take a moment to think about the most appropriate actions to take. You already know that there is no way to keep track of everything that you've ever produced on the internet, for the reasons already mentioned. Once you are aware of this, you can still put some limits on that lack of control, asking yourself what deserves to be saved and what should be deleted. In order to do this you need to backtrack and make an inventory of all of the accounts you've opened over the years, deciding which ones should remain active. This inventory could be started by searching through your emails, checking for traces of all of the other connected accounts in order to analyze them and begin the selection. Obviously, you have to follow the official procedures for deleting an account very carefully, even to the point of reading the contractual conditions you have agreed to—something hardly anyone ever does.

If you have opted for a digital cremation of your content after you die, you have to arrange things so that no one has the information necessary to access your various accounts. You need to establish in advance—wherever possible, like it is with the social networks—that your accounts will be deleted upon your death. Then, you store your digital assets on a disk or another type of physical storage device. Once you have chosen where to store these assets, you lock them by using encryption software and don't let anyone else have your decoding keys. Given that the complete cremation of the material you have produced and saved online is not possible, you must clearly express to your relatives that, upon your death, you would at least like to have the content related to your identity de-referenced. This means that you can ask for online search engines to eliminate any links to personal content that are no longer relevant from their results pages. The most notable case related to this is the 2014 ruling regarding a Spanish citizen who used Europe's privacy laws to request the removal of links that turned up in search results when someone Googled his name. Some of these links sent searchers back to the pages of local newspapers that tied his name to the auction notice for his home, which had been repossessed sixteen years earlier. It was being sold to cover his tax debt. He felt that this information, no longer relevant as he had paid off his debts during those sixteen years, now violated his privacy. The judges upheld his claim and ruled that an individual could ask search engines to de-index content considered irrelevant, independent of the fact that it was still available online.[10]

If you would like to leave your digital memories to posterity, first you need to make a record of the access information (usernames and passwords) for all of your active accounts. Then you should choose a trustworthy person in advance, charged with the task of keeping this information so that—in the event of your death—your relatives can have access to the legacy you want them to inherit. Not taking these precautions means risking a repeat of what happened when the thirteen-year-old Italian boy, Dama, died in 2015 from an osteosarcoma (a malignant type of bone tumor). His father, who didn't have the access codes to his son's phone, pleaded with Apple to get access to his content, so that he could keep the final words and images preserved on the phone as a memorial. Even though Dama had backed up his data, and his father was in possession of that, the very last interactions that had taken place on his mobile phone hadn't been saved elsewhere. Like the case in Berlin where the parents petitioned Facebook to access their deceased daughter's account, Apple prevented the father from accessing his son's phone, using the argument that they were protecting the user's privacy. The father claimed that Apple had, in fact, denied his right to these memories of his son.

There are currently many services that, keeping Dama's father's experience in mind and taking Sartre's words—"The unique characteristic of a dead life is that it is a life of which the Other makes himself the guardian"[11]—seriously, offer support to those who want to create their own digital legacy. This includes the username and password access already mentioned, but also all of the other digital objects produced over a lifetime: photographs, written texts, videos, playlists of favorite songs, and so on.

One example is eMemory (https://www.ememory.it/), an Italian website that aims to make a connection between memory and digital selection. They combine two purposes, that of determining and protecting an individual's digital legacy with that of educating them about the ecological use of the internet. This is why eMemory looks like a digital home within which each person carves out a space, building and preserving their memories. One of the company's central tenets is the idea that memory involves selection and that there is no freedom without memory. Their theoretical starting point is an observation of the overabundance of information and the resulting senseless accumulation of digital material that lacks any selection criteria. This accumulation of content means that the significant aspects of your personhood risk being lost because you are completely submerged in the material you have produced, shared, and then saved. With this in mind, eMemory supplies an online space—partly free and partly for a fee—where users can select and catalog their own digital legacy, with different levels of privacy. In addition, users can also save their user names and passwords to various accounts, creating a kind of digital will that will be delivered to the people specified upon the user's death. The interesting aspect of eMemory is its quality as an archive: any content stored in it can be accompanied by written or recorded information, which offers a detailed description of the corresponding experience, strengthening the memory of the person who is no longer there.

Like eMemory, BoxTomorrow (www.boxtomorrow.com) offers a logical approach to preparing your digital will. You sign up for the service and build a kind of virtual box in which you can put your photographs and documents, along with files containing your usernames and passwords for important websites. Upon your death, your beneficiaries can open the virtual box and access the material you've bequeathed to them. The American website Memories (https://www.memories.com/), created by two Israeli brothers living in the United States., is meant to help you curate your memories. It offers a variety of privacy plans and also helps preserve your memories of the deceased. The French website GrantWill (https://www.grantwill.com/en/) even goes so far as to describe itself as the first social network for the dead, although the services are more or less in line with the others previously described. GrantWill provides a digital safe for storing personal, administrative, and business data. In addition, the company offers a service that will send personalized messages to friends and relatives, and communicate important, private information to those who have been chosen in advance as your digital identity managers once you have died. The website states: "Don't be afraid, we will all die one day. Nobody lives forever. Nowadays we live faster than before, time flies. This can make things difficult for our relatives and loved ones."

Another interesting website is Elysway (http://www.elysway.com), which calls itself the Facebook of the dead. Started in autumn of 2014 and with an interface available in five languages, Elysway offers a variety of services. First, the user creates a page that is like a Facebook page. Here, friends, relatives, and acquaintances—called "passengers"—can post videos, photos, and images of the deceased; instead of a "like," they can post "my condolences" below the content. The deceased is called a "star" and their page features a biography and is meant to keep that individual's memory alive. The person who creates and manages the "star page," which is to say the profile of the deceased, is called the "star angel." This person manages all of the information posted by passengers and other angels.

Other services focus on farewell videos. The U.S. website SafeBeyond (www.safebeyond.com) offers users the ability to produce videos to leave to their loved ones. These videos, according to the precise instructions of the person who made them, will be delivered to the intended recipients at a meaningful moment in their lives (if desired, together with passwords and other elements of a digital legacy). The presentation video for the service shows a situation where the terminally ill father of an eight-year-old girl is making a video, while the girl—unaware—is playing on the beach. In the following scenes we see his grown daughter on her wedding day as she receives her father's video message expressing his sadness at not being there along with his assurances of how proud he is of her and that he is with her in spirit. The home page also quotes the famous words of Steve Jobs, who stresses that death is one of life's best "inventions," functioning as an agent of change that clears out the old and makes way for the new, despite the fact that no one really wants to die. Much like SafeBeyond, If I Die (an app mentioned in the introduction) offers, in addition to farewell videos, a contest called "If I Die First." The message of the first user to die, out of all the users who choose to "participate" by leaving an *if i die 1st* message, will be "awarded" global exposure estimated at 200 million people through Facebook, Mashable, and various other media outlets.

Finally, the Italian website Memori (https://getmemori
.com) is worth mentioning. Conceived by the homony-
mous company Memory Srl, which specializes in language
recognition projects, voice interfaces, and mobile and IoT
(Internet of Things) platforms, Memori is an interactive digital memory box for human memories. It's a box where you
can enter written text, images, and audiovisual recordings,
each one of which is connected to a memory, an object, or a
specific question. Once plugged in, this box has an interface
with which users can interact. This allows you to associate
certain objects with specific people. Suppose I associate this
object with a close relative. A close relative just places the
object on top of the Memori box and the box will recognize them, say hello, and then speak with them as if you
yourself were speaking. The basic assumption of all of these
projects, and there are many others, is that the power death
exercises and the place it occupies in our lives, is contained
in the power of memory. It is from memory that we draw the
strength to enrich our life path, to grow—and to enhance
our way of thinking. Above all, memory can intensify the
echo of those who are no longer with us in our own lives and
help us prepare our own "echo" in the lives of others when
it's our turn to leave. Today, digital culture offers memory
(which is to say the spiritual flow between the hereafter and
the here-and-now) the ability to give a tangible and personal
voice to that echo. The digital body can become a depository
for intimate bonds, the consoling voice able to vest memory
with the trappings that made the relationship each one of us
has had with our loved one unique, for better and for worse.

Ultimately, it should be pointed out that almost all of the services mentioned guarantee that they will create a copy of the material shared, so that a copy can be saved on your own computer or printed, and therefore "physically" saved. This option is strongly recommended because digital memory is extremely fragile. Your digital legacy risks being utterly lost as soon as the format, or hardware on which it is stored, becomes obsolete.

A few years ago Google's vice president, Vinto Cerf, caused a sensation during the annual meeting of the American Association for the Advancement of Science when he claimed it was quite probable that the document formats we currently use would become obsolete, and consequently unreadable. Not being aware of this and therefore not looking for concrete solutions means running the risk of producing a genuine "digital desert," in which future historians will be unable to find documents from our era. Not to put too fine a point on it, he pointed out that in the 1980s we were saving our documents on floppy disks and killing video game aliens with Quickfire II joysticks—items that have become museum pieces in the arc of a few decades. Just think back to the first emails. The content that was generated in early versions of Microsoft Outlook is gone for good, because at the time we were not aware of the necessity of saving the content we produced.

Considering these issues, the paradox of digital archives becomes even more evident. While we are digitizing our assets, thinking that it's the best way to preserve them over time, we have not considered that an analogue copy of our material—for example, a printed photograph—could last longer than a digital one.

Abby Smith Rumsey, in her book *When We Are No More: How Digital Memory Is Shaping Our Future*, emphasizes the unimaginable fragility of the digital storage devices to which we are entrusting our memories.[12] Today, our cultural memory is integrated with a system of complex technologies that are constantly being redefined and implemented. And this means that any change to the system threatens to make our saved content illegible. A paper book can last for hundreds of years; it's enough to make sure that it is kept in the right environment and there are eyes available to read it. In contrast, PDF files depend on codes and data that can quickly become obsolete, running the risk of never being read again.

In turn, Luciano Floridi believes that our digital memory is as volatile as our oral culture, if not more so. "Memory is not just a question of storage and efficient management; it is also a matter of careful curation of significant differences, and hence of the stable sedimentation of the past as an ordered series of changes, two historical processes that are now seriously at risk."[13] There are millions of abandoned pages on the Internet; because they are constantly being updated, websites are not saving any remnants of their past. Wayback Machine aside, the saving of a document means erasing the preceding versions. As the years go by, hard disks and other digital supports risk deteriorating, as do CDs and DVDs when compared with the longevity of vinyl. Floridi thinks that, because of continuous technological evolutions, big data will age and die, resulting in the loss of an impressive amount of material that has been digitally archived. In highlighting this apocalyptic scenario, he takes us back to where we started: our awareness of how fragile digital memory is must have an impact on our subjective ability to select from the immense amount of digital material produced and encourage us to develop a fuller sense of responsibility for the way we construct and maintain our selected memories. Whatever action we chose to take, we must carefully consider digital culture's perpetual, contradictory oscillations between the data that risks remaining on the web for all eternity (whether we like it or not) and the data that is in danger of being lost forever.

In my view, this also involves a focused consideration of our own mortality, and of the certainty that we are not meant to live forever. This is why all of the memories that we produce, if they are not organized and curated, will disappear into the general flow of the world wide web and create more suffering for those who loved us and who have survived us. Digital inheritance ultimately opens up a series of controversial legal scenarios in terms of the right to be forgotten and personal privacy. In the end, the archival environment, considering how many traces we leave online, is also a thanatological one. If I have to plan out how to deal with my memories and recollections so that they will not end up completely lost or anarchically dispersed around the internet, I must also consider that my life will not go on forever and that all I have produced will last beyond my physical death, continuing to impact the world of the living.

Digitizing Memories: Hi-Tech Cemeteries

In his book *Visioni digitali: Video, web e nuove tecnologie* (*Digital Visions: Video, Web and New Technologies*), Simone Arcagni describes the characteristics of today's technological innovations and the revolution that has taken place in terms of how we view images. He points out multiple times how the Web 3.0 is a "'pervasive' system that brings together objects, people, and machines into one, vast, and continually expanding universe of communication, which can be accessed through the screens on a variety of devices."[14] He also highlights the integration between these increasingly powerful interfaces and an audiovisual experience that encompasses both thought and communication.

The pervasive nature of a system that makes objects, people and machines indistinguishable from one another (within the context of a worldview in which online and off-line mirror each other) is also bringing fundamental changes to our funeral rites. The disruptive presence of death in the digital environment, where it is integrated with the various life experiences and the immense amount of memorabilia created by each individual user, has had an effect on the kind of innovations that are beginning to mark an evolutionary change in cemeteries. In particular, the progressive digitalization of these locations goes hand in hand with the commemoration of the dead on social networks and, in some ways, represents a meaningful connection with projects like MyDeathSpace. There is an increasingly direct link between how we think about cemeteries and the pervasiveness of communication and storytelling in the world around us (especially on social networks like Facebook, Twitter, Instagram, etc.). This connection has provoked a radical rethinking of headstones and the type of memory we associate with them. In other words, digital culture stands between "retrospective memory," which keeps the dead present for the living as a way of recognizing their importance to the group and reaffirming the unity and image of its broader culture, and "prospective memory," which is based on the specific ways in which the deceased is unforgettable (fame, achievements, etc.).[15] This creates an unprecedented integration of these two types of memory in new funeral practices.

When we go to the cemetery, we wander through a forest of headstones and other grave markers. On these markers we find the birth and death dates of the deceased, perhaps accompanied by a brief epitaph and a succinct description of their achievements if that person has played a meaningful role in society. This brings to mind two characters from the Italian film *Bianco, Rosso e Verdone* (1981), Mimmo and his grandmother. The two of them are in a cemetery looking for the headstone of someone whose name they cannot remember—"... a headstone with a last name like *Soriso, Rise, Risata* (Smile, Laughed, Laughing), like *Me vie' da ride* (It makes me laugh)?"[16]—and it is this forgetfulness that leads them to begin looking at other headstones and wondering about those buried there. Today, these kinds of questions are beginning to find answers in businesses that aim to use

digital culture to enhance the level of biographical information available on an individual's tombstone.

The first solution, which brings together funeral practices with digital culture, involves applying a QR code to a
headstone. QR is short for Quick Response code; this two-
dimensional barcode is made up of black squares arranged
in a square grid on a white background in such a way that it
is personalized and exclusively dedicated to a deceased individual. It can be used to store memories (songs, stories, anecdotes, photographs, etc.) that are usually meant to be viewed
on a smartphone. These can be bonded to the stone with
an adhesive that will withstand all kinds of weather. Each
QR code is linked to the Facebook profile of the deceased
or, more commonly, to a web page where friends and family create that person's personal biography, adding their own
memories, anecdotes, and images. By using the QR reader on
a tablet or smartphone, the linked information (the biography of the deceased) can then be read. Sometimes access is
public while in other cases access is available only to authorized users.

In the United States and Great Britain, this practice is
widespread. The first QR codes on headstones were tried
out in Philadelphia and Seattle. In the latter city, the company Living Headstones has kept a step ahead of the com-
petition, offering to combine traditional stone markers with
new, innovative technologies, in a way that does not involve
any extra costs. The only exception is an eighty-dollar fee if
family members would like to update an existing headstone.
The Chester Pearce cemeteries in the English town of Poole,

and those of Roskilde in Denmark, are among the first in Europe to have tried this new technology.

When it comes to QR codes on headstones, one of the most comprehensive services is offered by Cloud Memorials (http://www.cloudmemorials.ph/login). This site invites those who knew the deceased to create a Cloud Biography on the website. This personal biography of the deceased can be continually augmented by the addition of personal testimonials, photographs, and anecdotes provided by those close to them. Once the Cloud Biography has been established, the QR code will be placed on the tombstone of the deceased so that their biography can be read by those visiting the cemetery. Cloud Memorials also allows users to search the biographies for people they know. Access is public and the names of the deceased are in alphabetical order. The effect is similar to that of MyDeathSpace: a virtual cemetery, full of stories about special moments. For example, on the page of a young woman who died when she was only twenty years old, we see a photo of her, a description of her brief life and her personality, along with information about her activities at school and work. She has twenty-one followers, many of whom have posted a photograph that included her. Every caption is an opportunity to describe what is happening in the photo. So we see her in the swimming pool, at the disco, at the local museum, and with her friends at a party. One contact, sharing a special photo, points out that he had forgotten that he had the photograph;this is followed by an exclamation of laughter ("Hahaha!") and the sad comment that this was probably the last time they had hung out together. Clearly when he found it, he felt the desire to share it with the young woman's loved ones. All of this information can be viewed either directly on the Cloud Memorials website or, by scanning the QR code on a headstone in the cemetery.

In Italy, this phenomenon is starting to catch on. In Cinisello Balsamo, a suburb of Milan, the first official digital gravestone will soon be installed. This involves the application of a QR code on the marble headstone in the local cemetery. In a town in the Italian province of Treviso, a woman chose to place a QR code on the tombstone of her boyfriend on her own initiative. This code links cemetery visitors to his personal blog where, among other things, he talks about the cancer that lead to his death.

It's very likely that, in the coming years, applying QR codes to gravestones will become common practice worldwide, making cemeteries a true resource for biographical information about the dead. The main downside is maintenance: that means constantly checking to make sure that the website linked to the code is functional, that the cemeteries have active data and Wi-Fi connections, and that the systems do not become obsolete as digital and computer technologies evolve. At any rate, it's enough to keep combining innovation with tradition, so that gravestones will be able to furnish the necessary information about the deceased even in the absence of digital services. It's also important to back up the biographical material in a format that is guaranteed to last. After all, it has always been possible for the memory of the deceased to fall by the wayside, even with traditional ways of marking their burial location. In many parts of the world, bodies are subject to exhumation or removal because the contract with the cemetery was not "in perpetuity." If there is no one to represent the interests of the family or of the deceased, the remains are removed to a communal ossuary and risk meeting the same fate as websites that are no longer maintained and cease to function.

The Japanese cemetery of Ruriden (http://www.ruriden .jp), associated with the Kōkoku-ji temple in central Tokyo, has gone well beyond the concept of QR codes on tombstones. This cemetery, actually a columbarium, contains more than two thousand glass Buddha statuettes, all illuminated by LED lights that change color and pattern according to the season and the weather. The statuettes are placed inside a transparent glass display, a floor-to-ceiling grid made up of glass boxes, each of which represents a deceased individual, from a nine-month-old child to a hundred-year-old woman. Ruriden works like this: the deceased is cremated and their ashes are then kept in a locker behind the wall. Each deceased person is assigned a specific statue; which is then linked to a smart card containing all of their basic personal information. A relative or visitor uses the smart card to access the cemetery and to illuminate the Buddha statue that corresponds to their loved one, distinguishing it from the others. This incredibly futuristic cemetery, from the structure to the interior lights, was commissioned by Kōkoku-ji's head priest in order to offer a reasonably priced solution to people who were single, childless, or just couldn't afford a family tomb (which can cost up to forty-thousand euros). The much more reasonable costs at Ruriden include that of the Buddha statuette and a modest annual fee for maintenance and storage of an individual's ashes for thirty-three years. The statuettes are symbolically thought of as companions in a high-tech afterlife, giving people who die without family the sense that they will be surrounded by others like them and therefore not "alone." Another one of Japan's high-tech cemeteries, Rurikoin Temple, also has screens that display commemorative digital photo albums of the deceased. Clearly Japan is at the forefront of digital funeral practices—indeed some rites are already being performed by robot priests—and this presages a near future in which holographic representations of the dead can be used, accompanied by prerecorded dialogue that will give the impression of being able to speak with the dead whenever we visit them at the cemetery.

The idea of digitizing funerals and the Japanese goal of making holograms of the deceased have inspired the Hereafter Institute that, in concert with the Los Angeles County Museum of Art (LACMA), has worked extensively with technological practices in the broad sense as well as specifically with futuristic funerals and cemeteries. The work done by this American institution is extremely high-tech, to the point where it seems out of place to those who are attached to a traditional concept of funeral rites. For example, if up until now it has been common practice for some people to wear a locket or a pendant with a small photograph of their deceased loved one, Hereafter offers an alternative "locket" that, instead of a still photo, displays videos of the deceased. Such an invention is perfectly in line with ongoing changes in how we communicate. The result—preserving the memory of the dead—is the same as that of a traditional locket; the only change is in the technology used to represent the deceased. Hereafter also offers those who are grieving photo reconstructions and a 3D video in a virtual room, which has the name of the deceased written on the door. Once they have donned the virtual reality goggles and entered the room, the user finds an artificial reproduction of the deceased, waiting to interact. The managers of the Hereafter Institute argue that as time passes, people will become increasingly interested in replacing traditional gravesites with digital memorials. The goal is to take control of the present, reestablishing the rituals and norms of mourning and dealing with the trauma of loss.

It's clear that the posthumous interaction offered to relatives of the deceased by the Hereafter Institute's project is similar to that created by chatbots, Counterparts and holograms. However, unlike the artificial dialogue with chatbots and holograms—which can take place anywhere that a mobile device will go—this type of interaction is limited to the place where the remains of a loved one are buried. So even if virtual communication can still upset the delicate emotional balance of those who have suffered a loss, the specific location has a clear symbolic link to the separate worlds of the living and the dead. Visitors to a gravesite usually "talk" to the deceased; Hereafter offers the possibility of receiving a consolatory response.

There is also a more informal concept of the cemetery available for mobile devices—with applications like RipCemetery and iRIP—that an individual can use to create a family cemetery on their own smartphone, customizing it with a variety of graphics. Friends and family members can share their memories, adding posts, photographs, and virtual flowers to the gravestone. By creating a kind of virtual cemetery for mobile devices, RipCemetery offers the following options: it allows every user to see who else has visited the family gravestone, to share files in digital format, and to save time for those who might find it difficult to physically visit the cemetery. In explaining the underlying idea, the founders emphasize the fact that our lives are increasingly experienced online and the demands on our time have also increased. They also note that visiting a cemetery to work through emotions is something that is mostly done by the elderly in our society. Grief and mourning is something that typically happens at home, and we are already used to finding refuge behind the screen of a computer, tablet, or smartphone as a way of coping with our grief.

Livestreaming and Selfies at Funerals

Intuitively, the concept of a family cemetery on a digital device leads easily to the idea of *livestreaming funerals*. All you need to do before the funeral is set up a digital video system that supports streaming video in a part of the chapel (or other location) that is high enough to capture the most important aspects of the event. The funeral can then be livestreamed online, and displayed on PC, tablet, or smart-phone screens.

The livestreamed funeral, which can be attended by the close friends and family members of the deceased—supplied with the appropriate access codes in advance—was conceived as a useful innovation to cope with a world in which a substantial number of people are emigrating from one place to another. Not everyone has the time, financial resources, or flexibility in their work schedule to physically attend the funeral of a loved one when it is being held in another part of the world. If they can watch the funeral at home, on their own computer, it's better than not attending it at all and exacerbating the pain they are going through. Generally speaking, once the livestreaming of the ceremony is over, there is no way to watch it again; after all, we're not talking about a football match or a concert. However, in many countries there are services that will make a video of the event and provide clients with a permanent copy. One of the first companies to offer livestreaming of funerals in Europe was the Ireland-based Funerals Live (http://funeralslive.ie), which was founded following the widespread emigration of Irish citizens due to the economic crisis. Having this service available means that Irish people who are far from home do not have to spend all of their savings on plane tickets to return to Ireland for the funeral of a close friend or family member.

In China, during the Qingming Festival (a traditional Chinese festival similar to the Christian All Saints' Day), people usually visit the cemetery to commemorate the dead and clean their graves. During this event, the Yuhuatai Martyrs' Cemetery in Nanjing City now makes it possible for those who cannot attend for work reasons to do so online, using one of China's most popular social media platforms, WeChat. For a fee, cemetery workers will perform the traditional rites for the dearly departed and livestream the event to the absent relative. The relative just has to register online and make the payment in order to receive their personal password to watch the ritual being carried out on their behalf. Not surprisingly, this has generated quite a bit of controversy and criticism in China.

The ongoing discussion about whether or not it is appropriate to livestream funerals arouses strong emotions. Some welcome the positive aspects, especially in terms of reducing costs but also because it allows those friends and family members who cannot travel to participate in an important family ritual, albeit indirectly. Others focus on the negative aspects because they feel that being physically present at the funeral is crucial to the grieving process. The actual corpse is proof positive that an individual has died, tangible evidence that they have left the community of the living and are forever consigned to another place. For this reason, many feel that experiencing this ritual online defeats its purpose, as it no longer serves the function of offering physical proof of death, and may create psychological problems for those who have suffered the loss. Watching a funeral onscreen could easily distance people from an authentic experience of the death of their loved one. These are valid considerations, even if those who are taking advantage of streaming services probably would not have been able to attend a funeral at all if they were required to be physically present at a church or cemetery. Furthermore, in Western countries—where funerals are often marked by the prevalence of a gloomy and sorrowful atmosphere—there are those who prefer not to take part, choosing to deal with the pain of separation privately. This is another instance in which the option of a livestreamed funeral could represent a reasonable compromise between the need to be present during the funeral and the desire to grieve in private.

The livestreaming of funerals is probably one of the most innovative ideas around today. It brings the rediscovery of death as part of everyday life to the fore, emphasizing its communicative and theatrical qualities. This practice is linked, in some ways, to the popular trend of taking selfies at funerals, either alone or with the body of the deceased at an open casket service.

In 2013 there was an online blog, *Selfies at Funerals* (http://selfiesatfunerals.tumblr.com/) that collected funeral selfies, mostly taken by adolescents or young adults during funerals and (primarily) posted on Instagram. Sad expressions and funeral homes typically appeared in the foreground, but then there were also snaps where people were sticking out their tongues, young girls in surprisingly skimpy dresses posing like fashion models, group photos in front of the coffin, and so on. All of this accompanied by captions that expressed sadness and pain at the loss of a grandfather, aunt, or dear friend. If you search the hashtag #funeral on Instagram, you'll find a world of photographic wonder at your fingertips. These photos show black humor, funeral memorials, irreverence, and superficiality, all jumbled together in a bizarre mix of fiction and reality. Sometimes the hashtag is just being used as a metaphor for a particularly unfortunate moment in someone's day (a failed exam or the end of a relationship), but sometimes it is marking an actual funeral. Many photographs also feature the corpse of the deceased stretched out in the casket, paired with comments that combine hilarity and pain. In Great Britain the issue of funeral selfies made the daily papers, which published a survey indicating that a third of mourners admitted having taken one. Many funeral parlors and funeral directors have felt it necessary to try to regulate this practice so that it's done in a way that isn't insensitive or offensive to the family of the deceased. In 2013 former British prime minister David Cameron caused a storm of controversy when he agreed to Danish prime minister Helle Thorning-Schmidt's request to snap a selfie together with former U.S. president Barack Obama, during Nelson Mandela's memorial service.

Observing these photographs carefully, the viewer is at first understandably dismayed, guided by the idea that every selfie expresses the superficiality of those who, addicted to compulsively narcissistic self-portraiture, seem to have lost sight of the atmosphere of remembrance and silence deemed appropriate at funerals. And this idea certainly has its basis in fact. On the other hand, it's simplistic to view the practice of taking selfies at funerals as yet another negative consequence of the prevalence of social networks.

First, it's important to remember that preserving the image of the cadaver, even if it is generally seen as macabre and offensive in contemporary Western culture, was a widespread practice in the past and is still part of some Eastern cultures today. Just consider the Ma'nene death ritual of the Tana Toraja people on the Indonesian island of Sulawesi. During this ceremony the dead are taken out of their graves, cleaned, dressed in fresh clothes, and photographed together with the family. Second, each individual has their own, specific way of relating, emotionally and psychologically, to the funeral ritual, to their deceased loved one, and to the practice of taking selfies—so it's not appropriate to generalize.

Therefore, selfies taken during a funeral are not unlike public commemorations on Facebook. Both express the desire to participate in an online group when someone we know dies and an attempt to empathize with others. In many cases, the choice to make a self-portrait, in this specifically painful situation, can be understood as a desire to share the experience with friends and acquaintances; therefore, the focus is on the person who has suffered the loss rather than on the person who has died. In other words, there is an attempt to use the current communication system, in particular the therapeutic function of images, as a way of protecting oneself from feeling isolated when dealing with the pain brought on by the end of a loved one's life. Snapping a selfie at a funeral, whether the expression is humorous or sad, allows the subject to ask for and receive empathy from others, to defuse the drama of a situation filled with difficult emotions for a few seconds, and to normalize death itself.

If, as Stacey Pitsillides says, death is a part of life and life
has become digital, then digitizing funerals and giving them
a place in our everyday digital life through an image—at the
cemetery, in the mortuary, or during a funeral in church—is
simply a way of recognizing that, in addition to having fun
vacations, celebrating birthdays, and singing at concerts, we
die. And we need to be reminded of that fact and have the
fortitude to integrate this inevitable moment into the fabric
of our daily lives. There is nothing wrong with the photographs you see on Instagram or on the *Selfies at Funerals* blog,
as long as this is not used as to justify superficial behavior
or conduct that is offensive to others. But it is important to
remember that the risk of superficiality or offensive behavior
is a normal part of the off-line world as well, and it has nothing to do with the influence of digital culture on how we live
and interact with the world around us.[17]

Afterword

In Javier Marías's novel *Tomorrow in the Battle Think on Me*, when Victor finds himself in the bedroom of his recently deceased lover, Marta, who, moments earlier, died in his arms, one of the first thoughts that crosses his mind is that her death seems less definitive because he was also present in the same room when she was alive, just a few seconds earlier. Up until the moment of her death, they had been having a passionate exchange in that same bedroom and were in the verge of making love. The sudden death of one of the two people placed the other in a somewhat surreal situation. The woman's crumpled skirt next to the bed still has an explanation, a history, a reason, because Victor is a witness to the fact that she was wearing it. He saw the way she took off the shoes that are now lying docilely on the floor. His presence, watching as his lover passed from life to death, in some way seems to prolong the life that has ended, because Victor is an eyewitness to the defining moment. She was so *alive* just moments earlier. And yet, on the other hand, he seems to have a better understanding of the meaning of death, gained from the very rare occurrence of finding himself with a woman who has died in his arms, right in front of his eyes.

The reflections that Javier Marías articulates in his novel are very useful for understanding the relationship between digital culture and death, as it has been described in this book. The feeling that you get when you look at a dead friend's Facebook page is similar to what Víctor was feeling in his lover's bedroom. A Facebook page, where people have conversations, and exchange photographs and videos, is an objective witness to an authentic life, just as much as a bedroom is. Each detail of a deceased user's timeline takes on the role of an explanation, a history, a reason, because each one of that person's friends and relatives is a demonstration of the fact that individual was alive.

Everything we find on the Facebook page of an individual who has died puts us in a position that makes it difficult to believe we are looking at a life that has come to an end. In fact, social networks are the perfect place for continuous interaction with others, for the existence of interconnected identities, which live by virtue of dialogue exchanged with others and individual narratives that work together to tell our stories. On the other hand, there is currently no more direct way of experiencing death: the sudden silence, not having had the chance to say goodbye, the last post—these are many of the elements that make this interruption, which clearly defines the passage from life to death, visible. On social networking sites death is recorded, clearly and definitively.

So this is the fundamental role that digital culture has unwittingly taken on relative to our uneven relationship with death, after decades of sociocultural erasure in the West. The internet, starting with social networks, creates the opportunity for each one of us to come to terms with our own mortality. These social networks also give death education an additional tool for instructing people about how to manage their lives, helping make them aware that this existence is not meant to last forever. The internet offers us an occasion for putting the grieving process back into a protected, community context, for rationally considering the fate of our identity when we are no longer alive, and for reflecting more attentively on the fragility of life. If we don't take advantage of this opportunity, we risk misrepresenting the image of death and the dead on the screens of our computers and mobile devices. If we let that happen, the digital sphere will become yet one more place to dramatically trivialize the meaning of death and even to avoid it, pretending that it has not happened. Effectively, this is the result of all those projects (chatbots, Counterparts, and holograms) that aim to extend the identity of the individual, who "embodied" it during their lifetime, beyond their actual death.

Thus, the development of interdisciplinary studies on the topic of digital death is key from many points of view, precisely because the significance of death's role (and how valuable it is) in the context of digital platforms is not yet clearly understood. In my view, what matters most is understanding that there is no radical contrast between the online and off-line dimensions; therefore, all our behavior on the internet responds to requirements and needs that are also part of our external world. Every innovation, which at first glance seems exaggeratedly high-tech, actually represents an attempt to use what the modern world of information and communication has to offer in order to address our fears and concerns about the end of life.

Ultimately, with this book I wanted to explore a new dimension of our current lives, one that will become increasingly intrusive over time. One that requires the conscious and reasoned ability of human beings to build their own defensive barriers, so that they can avoid the disorientation that—all too often—is generated by the death of a loved one and by the thought that eternity belongs to the realm of science fiction rather than to our everyday lives.

Acknowledgments

My studies on digital death have taken place over the last several years through research projects, conferences, seminars, and lectures throughout Italy. I was lucky enough to encounter professionals with a broad range of perspectives, each one of whom has greatly enriched my thought process.

First of all, I would like to offer my heartfelt thanks to Roberto Gilodi, Michele Luzzatto, and the editors at Bollati Boringhieri, who believed in this project and made the writing of this book possible.

I would also like to thank Marina Sozzi and Infine Onlus of Turin, for the rich, intense and always engaging conversation that took shape in the blog *Si può dire morte* (You can say death).

I am deeply grateful to Ines Testoni and the Master's program "Death Studies & End of Life" offered by the University of Padua, which represents the best Italy has to offer in terms of death education and end of life studies.

I also thank all of those who have expressed interest, over the years, in my thanatological studies and with whom a variety of synergies have been created: Graziano Lingua and

Cespec of Cuneo, Alessandro De Cesaris, Lorenzo De Stefano and friends from NapoliFilosofica, the Nexa Center for Internet & Society of Turin's Polytechnic University, Giancarlo Lacchin and the Collegio of Milan, Raffaella Maiullo and the Piccolo Opificio Sociologico of Florence, Antonella Ursic and the Caffè Filosofico Trieste, Ana Cristina Vargas, Gisella Gramaglia and Turin's Ariodante Fabretti Foundation, and therefore: Giampiero Moretti, Alessia Zielo, Laura Campanello, Alessandra Santoro, Maurizio Guerri, Ubaldo Fadini, Roberto Marchesini, Leslie Cameron Curry, Gabriella Baptist, Giovanna Frongia, Roberto Borsa, Giovanni Ziccardi, Federico Vercellone, Gaetano Chiurazzi, Maurizio Balistreri, and Giovanni Leghissa.

Then, I thank the many friends and acquaintances who, like me, are deeply interested in the topic of digital death and have provided me with some fundamental insights over the years: Elena Benzo, Marta Montanaro, Silvia Maria Esposito, Chiara Falcitelli, Veronica Cavedagna, and Maria Angela Donna. It's impossible to mention everyone to whom I am grateful by name, but I'll pay for the beer the next time we meet.

I would also like to thank Ugo Ugazio for the meaningful philosophical dialogue that we have shared over the years. My last and most important thoughts turn to Nello and to the "heavy metal" lady of my life, Silvana; more than just a mother, she is energetic existential fuel. And finally Roberta, my soulmate whose iridescent imprint can be found in every line of this book.

Notes

Introduction

1. Kenneth Goldsmith, *Wasting Time on the Internet* (New York: Harper Perennial, 2016), 88. With the metaphor of the "random spider," Goldsmith is referring to a software program that travels the web locating and indexing websites for search engines.

2. Byunt-Chul Han, *Psychopolitics: Neoliberalism and New Technologies of Power* (London and New York: Verso Books, 2017), 55–66.

3. On the topic of death education, I recommend the comprehensive work of Ines Testoni, *L'ultima nascita. Psicologia del morire e "Death Education"* [The Last Birth. The Psychology of Dying and "Death Education"] (Turin, Italy: Bollati Boringhieri, 2015).

4. Atul Gawande, *Being Mortal: Medicine and What Matters in the End* (New York: Metropolitan Books, 2014).

5. The Australian research mentioned is the following: D. Rawlings et al., "Passed Away, Kicked the Bucket, Pushing Up Daisies: The Many Ways We Don't Talk about Death," in *The Conversation*, May 22, 2017, http://theconversation.com/passed-away-kicked-the-bucket -pushing-up-daisies-themany-ways-we-dont-talk-about-death-77085.

Regarding Alberta Ferrari's thoughts on the phrase "stroncato da un male incurabile," see http://ferrari.blogautore.espresso.repub blica.it/2014/12/23/stroncata-da-un-male-incurabile-appello-per -un-giornalismosanitariodifferente/.

6. This website is now a research portfolio, but the contents mentioned can be found in academic papers such as the following: Stacey Pitsillides, Mike Waller, and Duncan Fairfax, "Digital Death: The Role Data Plays in How We Are (Re)Membered," in *Digital Identity and Social Media*, ed. Steven Warburton and Stylianos Hatzipanagos (Hershey, PA: IGI Global, 2013), 75–90.

7. Luciano Floridi, *The Fourth Revolution: How the Infosphere Is Reshaping Human Reality* (Oxford, UK: Oxford University Press, 2014), 43.

8. Floridi, *The Fourth Revolution*, 94.

9. One of the books that best describes the Swedish practice of *Döstädning* is the following: M. Magnusson, *The Gentle Art of Swedish Death Cleaning: How to Free Yourself and Your Family from a Lifetime of Clutter* (New York: Simon & Schuster, 2018).

10. See Walter Benjamin, "The Storyteller," in *Illuminations*, English translation by Harry Zohn (New York: Mariner Books, 2019), 107–108.

11. Novalis, *Philosophical Writings*, English translation by Margaret Mahony Stoljar (Albany: State University of New York Press, 1997), 23.

12. Evan Carroll and John Romano, *Your Digital Afterlife: When Facebook, Flickr and Twitter Are Your Estate, What's Your Legacy?* (Berkeley, CA: New Riders, 2011), 10.

13. Charles Bukowski, *The Captain Is Out to Lunch and the Sailors Have Taken Over the Ship* (New York: Ecco, 2002), 13.

14. Vilém Flusser, *Into the Universe of Technical Images* (Minneapolis: University of Minnesota Press, 2011), 136.

15. Flusser, *Into the Universe of Technical Images*, 18.

16. Carla J. Sofka, "Social Support 'Internetworks,' Caskets for Sale, and More: Thanatology and the Information Superhighway," *Death Studies* 21, no. 6 (1997): 553.

17. See John Durham Peters, *Speaking into the Air: A History of the Idea of Communication* (Chicago: University of Chicago Press, 1999), 149.

18. Thomas Macho, "Immagini e morte: Il tempo della fotografia" [Images and Death: The Era of Photography], *Trópos: Rivista di ermeneutica e critica filosofica* 2, no. 9 (February 2016): 16.

19. Régis Debray, *Vita e morte dell'immagine: Uno storia dello sguardo in Occidente* [Life and Death of the Image: A History of the Western Gaze], Italian translation by A. Pinotti (Milan, Italy: Il castoro, 1998), 28.

20. Michel Serres, "*The Hermaphrodite*: A translation of Michel Serres's *L'Hermaphrodite*" (Paris: Flammarion, 1989), by Randolph Burks," https://www.academia.edu/36390023/The_Hermaphrodite_by_Michel_Serres.

See also Tony Walter, "Communication Media and the Dead. From the Stone Age to Facebook," *Mortality* 20, no. 3 (2015): 215–232.

21. Regarding this, see Hans Belting, *An Anthropology of Images: Picture, Medium, Body* (Princeton, NJ: Princeton University Press, 2014), 85.

22. Susan Sontag, *On Photography* (New York: RosettaBooks, LLC, 2005), 55.

23. R. Roland Barthes, *Camera Lucida: Reflections on Photography*, English translation by Richard Howard (New York: Farrar, Straus and Giroux, 1981), 79.

24. Barthes, *Camera Lucida*, 31–32.

25. Jacques Derrida and Bernard Stiegler, *Ecografie della television*, Italian translation by L. Chiesa (Milan, Italy: Cortina, 1997), 47.

26. Maurizio Ferraris, *Documentalità: Perché è necessario lasciar tracce* [Documentality: Why It Is Necessary to Leave Traces] (Rome-Bari, Italy: Laterza, 2009), 209.

27. Yuval Noah Harari, *Homo Deus: A Brief History of Tomorrow* (London: Harville Secker, 2016), 394–395.

28. See Simone Arcagni, *Visioni digitali: Video, web e nuove tecnologie* [Digital Visions: Video, Web and New Technologies] (Turin, Italy: Einaudi, 2017), 37.

29. Maurizio Ferraris, *Anima e iPad: E se l'automa fosse lo specchio dell'anima?* [Soul and iPad: What If Robots Were the Mirror of the Soul?] (Parma, Italy: Guanda, 2011), 153.

30. Georges Canguilhem, *Writings on Medicine*, English translation by S. Geroulanos and T. Meyers (New York: Fordham University Press, 2012), 41. Regarding the ideas of Jankélévitch, see V. Jankélévitch, *La morte* [Death], edited by E. L. Petrini, Italian translation by V. Zini (Turin, Italy: Einaudi, 2009), 77.

31. Regarding the concept of "posthumous interaction," see Vincius Carvalho Pereira and Cristiano Maciel, "The Internet Generation and the Posthumous Interaction," in *Digital Legacy and Interaction: Post-Mortem Issues* (New York: Springer, 2013), 65.

The citation of Baudrillard is taken from *The Perfect Crime*, English translation by Chris Turner (London: Verso, 1996), 47.

32. Günther Anders, *L'uomo è antiquato. 1: Considerazioni sull'anima nell'epoca della seconda rivoluzione industriale*, Italian translation by L. Dallapiccola (Turin, Italy: Bollati Boringhieri, 2007), 56.

33. Giovanni Ziccardi, *Il libro digitale dei morti: Memoria, lutto, eternità e oblio nell'era dei social network* [The Digital Book of the Dead: Memory, Mourning, Eternity and Oblivion in the Era of the Social Network] (Turin, Italy: UTET, 2017), 207.

34. C. S. Lewis, *A Grief Observed* (Canada: Ebook Samizdat, 2016), 9.

35. A clear definition of "digital immortality" can be found in Doug DeGroot, "Keeping Our People Alive: The Role of Digital Immortality in Culture Preservation," in *Kulturelles Gedächtnisim im 21. Jahrhundert* [Cultural Preservation in the Twenty-First Century], edited by T.

Dreier and E. Euler, Tagungsband des internationalen Symposiums, 23 (Karlsruhe, Germany: Karlsruhe University Press, 2005), 33–56.

See also Debra J. Bassett, "Who Wants to Live Forever? Living, Dying and Grieving in Our Digital Society," *Social Sciences* 4, no. 4 (2015): 1127–1139.

1   Digital Immortality

1. Timothy Leary, with R. U. Sirius, *Design for Dying* (New York: HarperCollins, 1997), 7.

2. Gordon Bell and Jim Gray, "Digital Immortality," Technical Report MSR-TR-2000-101, Microsoft Research, October 1, 2000, https://www.microsoft.com/en-us/research/wp-content/uploads/2016/02/tr-2000-101.pdf.

3. Bell and Gray, "Digital Immortality."

4. The topic of the "technological singularity" is central to a book written by Ray Kurzweil, *The Singularity Is Near: When Humans Transcend Biology* (2006). A general explanation of the concept can be found in Zoltan Istvan, "Che cos'è la singolarità tecnologica?," *Motherboard*, Vice Media LLC, April 23, 2015, https://motherboard .vice.com/it/article/3dven5/singolarita-tecnologica.

5. For a full account of Roman Mazurenko's story, see Casey Newton, "Speak, Memory: When Her Best Friend Died, She Rebuilt Him Using Artificial Intelligence," *The Verge*, VOX media, October 6, 2016, https://www.theverge.com/a/luka-artificial-intelligence-memo rial-roman-mazurenko-bot.

For information regarding the Replika project, see Arielle Pardes, "The Emotional Chatbots Are Here to Probe Our Feelings," *Wired*, January 31, 2018, https://www.wired.com/story/replika-open-source/.

6. James Vlahos tells the full story of his invention in James Vlahos, "A Son's Race to Give His Dying Father Artificial Immor- tality," *Wired*, July 18, 2017, https://www.wired.com/story/a-sons -race-to-give-his-dying-father-artificial-immortality/.

See also James Vlahos, *Talk to Me: Amazon, Google, Apple and the Race for Voice-Controlled AI* (London: Random House Business Books, 2019), 251–277.

7. *The Day You Discard Your Body is online here:* https://marshallbrain .com/discard1.htm.

8. Jacques Derrida, *Ogni volta unica, la fine del mondo,* Italian translation by M. Zannini (Milan, Italy: Jaca Book, 2005), 11.

9. C. S. Lewis, *A Grief Observed* (Canada: Ebook Samizdat, 2016), 5.

10. Maurice Merleau-Ponty, *Phenomenology of Perception,* English translation by Colin Smith (London: Taylor and Francis e-Library, 2005), 93.

11. Roland Barthes, *Camera Lucida: Reflections on Photography,* English translation by Richard Howard (New York: Farrar, Straus and Giroux, 1981), 66.

12. Barthes, *Camera Lucida,* 66.

13. Barthes, *Camera Lucida,* 75.

14. Luigi Pirandello, "Colloqui con i personaggi," *Novelle per un anno* (Milan, Italy: Mondadori, 1951), 565.

15. See Martine Rothblatt, *Virtually Human: The Promise—and the Peril—of Digital Immortality* (New York: St. Martin's Press, 2014), 9–10.

16. Merleau-Ponty, *Phenomenology of Perception,* 412.

17. Merleau-Ponty, *Phenomenology of Perception,* 413.

18. Debra J. Bassett, "Who Wants to Live Forever? Living, Dying and Grieving in Our Digital Society," *Social Sciences* 4, no. 4 (November 20, 2015): 1134.

19. Marina Sozzi, *Sia fatta la mia volontà. Ripensare la morte per cambiare la vita* (Milan, Italy: Chiarelettere, 2014) 170.

20. Sozzi, *Sia fatta la mia volontà*.

21. Walter Benjamin, "The Storyteller," in *Illuminations*, English translation by Harry Zohn (New York: Mariner Books, 2019), 46.

22. Jorge Luis Borges, "The Immortal," in *Labyrinths* (London: Penguin Books Ltd, 2000), 146.

23. Patricia Wallace, *The Psychology of the Internet* (Cambridge, UK: Cambridge University Press, 2016), 32.

24. Manuel Castells, *La nascita della società in Rete*, Italian translation by L. Turchet (Milan, Italy: UBE Paperback, 2014), 516–517.

25. Jacques Derrida, *Specters of Marx: The State of the Debt, the Work of Mourning and the New International*, English translation by Peggy Kamuf (New York: Routledge Classics, 2006), 7.

26. Friedrich Wilhelm Joseph Schelling, *The Ages of the World*, English translation by Jason M. Wirth (Albany: State University of New York Press, 2000), 42.

27. Lewis, *A Grief Observed*, 11–12.

28. See Franco "Bifo" Berardi, *After the Future*, edited by Gary Genosko and Nicholas Thoburn (Oakland, CA: AK Press, 2011); Mark Fisher, *Ghosts of My Life: Writings on Depression, Hauntology and Lost Futures* (Winchester, UK: Zero Books, 2014).

29. Simon Reynolds, *Retromania: Pop Culture's Addiction to its Own Past* (New York: Faber and Faber, 2011), 56.

30. Reynolds, *Retromania*, 63.

2 Death and Social Networks

1. Jean Baudrillard, *Symbolic Exchange and Death (Theory, Culture & Society)*, English translation by Ian Hamilton Grant (Thousand Oaks, CA: Sage Publications, 1993), 126.

2. See Byung-Chul Han, *In the Swarm: Digital Prospects*, English translation by Erik Butler (Cambridge, MA: MIT Press, 2017), 11–12.

3. See Sherry Turkle, *Reclaiming Conversation: The Power of Talk in a Digital Age* (New York: Penguin, 2016).

4. Roland Barthes, *Mourning Diary*, English translation by Richard Howard (New York: Hill and Wang, 2010), 52.

5. Giuseppe Riva, Brenda K. Wiederhold, and Pietro Cipresso, *The Psychology of Social Networking Vol. 1: Personal Experience in Online Communities* (Berlin and Boston: De Gruyter, 2019), 10.

6. Eric Charles Steinhart, *Your Digital Afterlives: Computational Theories of Life after Death* (New York: Palgrave Macmillan, 2014), 2–3.

7. Maurizio Ferraris, *Anima e iPad: E se l'automa fosse lo specchio dell'anima?* (Parma, Italy: Guanda, 2011), 149.

8. Kenneth Goldsmith, *Wasting Time on the Internet* (New York: Harper Perennial, 2016), 96–97.

9. Eugène Minkowski, *Il tempo vissuto: Fenomenologia e psicopatologia*, Italian translation by G. Terzian, 2nd ed. (Turin, Italy: Einaudi, 2004), 136.

10. Walter Benjamin, "The Storyteller," in *Illuminations*, English translation by Harry Zohn (New York: Mariner Books, 2019), 39–40.

11. See Han, *In the Swarm: Digital Prospects*.

12. Susan Sontag, *On Photography* (New York: RosettaBooks, LLC, 2005), 15.

13. William R. Hobbs and Moira K. Burke, "Connective Recovery in Social Networks after the Death of a Friend," *Nature Human Behaviour* 1, article no. 0092 (April 24, 2017), https://www.nature.com/articles/s41562-017-0092.

14. Han, *In the Swarm: Digital Prospects*, 11.

15. See Kylie Veale, "Online Memorialisation: The Web as a Collective Memorial Landscape for Remembering the Dead," *Fibreculture*, Issue 3—General Issue (November 1, 2004), http://three.fibreculturejournal.org/fcj-014-online-memorialisation-the-web-as-a-collective-memorial-landscape-for-remembering-the-dead/.

16. Hans Belting, *An Anthropology of Images: Picture, Medium, Body* (Princeton, NJ: Princeton University Press, 2014) 60.

17. Rosi Braidotti, *Il postumano: La vita oltre l'individuo, oltre la specie, oltre la morte* [The Posthuman: Life beyond the Individual, beyond the Species, beyond Death] (Rome, Italy: DeriveApprodi, 2014), 140.

18. Giovanni Ziccardi, *Il libro digitale dei morti: Memoria, lutto, eternità e oblio nell'era dei social network* [The Digital Book of the Dead: Memory, Mourning, Eternity and Oblivion in the Era of the Social Network] (Turin, Italy: UTET, 2017), 174.

19. Ziccardi, *Il libro digitale dei morti*, 174–175.

20. Jan Assmann, *Cultural Memory and Early Civilization: Writing, Remembrance, and Political Imagination* (Cambridge, UK: Cambridge University Press, 2011), 47.

21. Cristina Giordana has recently published a book in Italy called *Portami lassù: Una storia vera di luce, amore e montagne* [Portami lassù: A True Story of Light, Love and Mountains] (Milan: Mondadori, 2019), in which she tells the story of her son doing exactly as she did in the Facebook account: that is, the story is told as if it were the son who wrote it.

22. Ziccardi, *Il libro digitale dei morti*, 62.

3   Digital Inheritance and Hi-Tech Funeral Rites

1. Dennis Klass, Phyllis R. Silverman, and Steven Nickman, *Continuing Bonds: New Understandings of Grief* (Washington, DC: Taylor & Francis, 1996).

2. Gustav Theodor Fechner, *The Little Book of Life after Death*, English translation by Mary C. Wadsworth (Boston: Little, Brown, & Company, 1905), 40.

3. George Saunders, *Lincoln in the Bardo: A Novel* (New York: Random House, 2017).

4. Franz Kafka, *Letters to Milena*, English translation by Philip Boehm (New York: Schocken Books, 1990), 223.

5. Giovanni Ziccardi, *Il libro digitale dei morti: Memoria, lutto, eternità e oblio nell'era dei social network* [The Digital Book of the Dead: Memory, Mourning, Eternity and Oblivion in the Era of the Social Network] (Turin, Italy: UTET, 2017), 126.

6. In 2019, American newspapers reported the story of Chastity Patterson, a 23-year-old girl from Newport, Arkansas. For four years, she had written messages to her dead father on WhatsApp. Her intention was to preserve her father's memory by telling him about the events in her life. But, unbeknownst to her, his phone number had been reassigned to another user. One day Chastity received this response: "Hi sweetheart, I am not your father, but I have been getting all your messages for the past 4 years. I look forward to your morning messages and your nightly updates. My name is Brad and I lost my daughter in a car wreck [in] August 2014 and your messages have kept me alive." Amanda Woods, "Woman Who Texted 'Dad' Every Day since His Death Gets a Surprise Reply," *New York Post*, October 28, 2019, https://nypost.com/2019/10/28/woman-who-texted-her-dad-every-day-since-his-death-gets-a-surprise-reply/.

7. See Adam Ostrom, "After Your Final Status Update," TED talk, July 2011, https://www.ted.com/talks/adam_ostrow_after_your_final_status_update?utm_campaign=social&utm_medium=referral&utm_source=facebook.com&utm_content=talk&utm_term=technology.

8. Jean Baudrillard, *The Perfect Crime*, English translation by Chris Turner (London: Verso, 1996), 25. On the topic of digital

inheritance, the following piece of investigative reporting by Salvatore Carrozzini was posted on the website HDBlog.it on January 28, 2018: "La mia identità digitale: Nascita e morte in un viaggio di 8 anni" [My Digital Identity: An 8-Year Voyage from Birth to Death]; it can be accessed at https://www.hdblog.it/2018/01/28/dati-personali-identitadigitale-guida-privacy/.

9. Jacques Derrida, *Specters of Marx: The State of the Debt, the Work of Mourning and the New International*, English translation by Peggy Kamuf (New York: Routledge Classics, 2006), 67–68.

10. Ziccardi, *Il libro digitale dei morti*, 72.

11. Jean-Paul Sartre, *Being and Nothingness*, English translation by Hazel E. Barnes (New York: Washington Square Press, 1956), 692–693.

12. See Abby Smith Rumsey, *When We Are No More: How Digital Memory Is Shaping Our Future* (New York: Bloomsbury Press, 2016).

13. Luciano Floridi, *The Fourth Revolution: How the Infosphere Is Reshaping Human Reality* (Oxford, UK: Oxford University Press, 2014), 18.

14. Simone Arcagni, *Visioni digitali: Video, web e nuove tecnologie* [Digital Visions: Video, Web and New Technologies] (Turin, Italy: Einaudi, 2017), 28.

15. The distinction between "retrospective memory" and "prospective memory" in reference to the memorialization of the dead is offered by Jan Assmann in *Cultural Memory and Early Civilization: Writing, Remembrance, and Political Imagination* (Cambridge, UK: Cambridge University Press, 2011), 45–46.

16. "Soriso, Rise, Risata" and "Me vie' da ride" are dialectal expressions of Roma citizens (in other words, this is Roma slang).

17. Regarding selfies during funerals, a very useful reference is James Meese et al., "Selfies at Funerals: Mourning and Presencing on Social Media Platforms," *International Journal of Communication* 9 (2015): 1818–1831.

Index